CICCHETTI

CICCHETTI

AND OTHER SMALL
ITALIAN PLATES TO SHARE

Lindy Wildsmith
Valentina Sforza

Race Point
PUBLISHING

Race Point
PUBLISHING

A division of Book Sales, Inc.
276 Fifth Avenue Suite 206
New York, New York 10001

RACE POINT PUBLISHING and the distinctive Race Point
Publishing logo are trademarks of Book Sales, Inc.

This 2013 edition published by Race Point Publishing by
arrangement with Quintet Publishing Limited

This book was conceived, designed, and produced by
Quintet Publishing Limited
6 Blundell Street
London N7 9BH
United Kingdom

COVER PHOTOGRAPHY Ian Garlick
FOOD STYLISTS Valentina Sforza and Antonella Tagliapietra
PHOTOGRAPHY Colin Dutton, 4 Corners Images
DESIGN Jacqui Caulton
EDITOR Margaret Swinson

ISBN-13: 978-1-937994-15-0

Printed in China

2 4 6 8 10 9 7 5 3 1

www.racepointpub.com

Contents

Introduction

The Venetians have made *cicchetti*—their version of *tapas*—into a culinary high-art form. Every Italian region has its own special snacks, and outside Venice these are not called *cicchetti* but *spuntini, piccoli cibi,* and *stuzzichini*. Italy is a wonderful place to eat not least because of the seasonality, variety, and the quality of the produce and the dishes. This is reflected in every aspect of Italian food including its finger food. To name just a few popular examples, Le Marche has olive *ascolane*, deep-fried stuffed queen olives. Rome has *suppli' di riso*, deep-fried balls of *risotto* with soft *mozzarella* or other fillings in the center. Tuscany has rich *crostini di fegatini*, or chicken liver toasts. Piedmont has heavily truffle-scented *crostini*, and Sicily has aromatic *panelle*, or chickpea fritters. Each little dish reflects its region's culinary traditions, cooking methods, produce, and ingredients. In fact, these *cicchetti* are often the best of the regions' specialties, simply made in miniature.

The book is therefore divided into two. The first half is written by Lindy Wildsmith and celebrates the traditions of Venetian *cicchetti*. It contains a selection of *cicchetti* recipes divided into sections on seafood, *crudo* (raw fish or meat), meat, fresh produce, cheese, *charcuterie* (prepared meats), and the *aperitifs* to serve with them. The second part of the book, written by Valentina Sforza, has extended the culinary journey around the other Italian regions to share some of the finest *stuzzichini* produced by *friggitori* (fried food stalls), bars, and *rosticcerie* (shops selling roasted meat) from Milan to Palermo.

Fresh produce, a crucial aspect of these recipes, is abundant in Italy. A visit to any food market is a treat for the senses. Stall after stall sells every kind of lettuce and salad leaves. Fruit and vegetables spill out over every street in a seemingly never-ending flow of commerce. Competition is rife, stalls stand shoulder to shoulder, and every trader vies for your attention.

Markets are noisy, bustling places at the heart of every *quartiere,* and business starts early in the morning. Since much of the produce is grown on smallholdings around the peripheries of towns and cities, it will have been harvested that day and still covered in dew.

Seasonality is still taken for granted in Italy. Although crops are grown under glass and plastic to ensure an early harvest, most growers are still small farmers. The taste and smell of their natural produce is far more important than the way it looks, and some of it is available for a short time only.

I was once in Siracusa, Sicily during the wild asparagus season in early spring. Every stall had its bucket of long, grassy spears. Every restaurant had asparagus on the menu, either as a *crostino*, *antipasto*, *primo*, or *secondo*, for the duration of the season, and then it disappeared for another 11 months. I may never be in Siracusa at that time again, but I will never forget the green, grassy flavor and tender texture of its wild asparagus.

Another example is the artichoke, which has many varieties that come and go through the season in Erbaria, Venice. Artichoke hearts play a leading role on *antipasto* menus nationwide. Cleaning an artichoke for the pot is very time-consuming. Market stall-holders stand around barrels from early morning, cutting and cleaning them for cooking. Each variety of artichoke makes its quiet debut to rapturous applause at some point in the season and then quietly takes a bow and disappears until the coming year.

Cicchetti

Anyone who has strolled around Venice in search of something to eat will have come across *cicchetti*. They are served in bars, *bàcari*, and other eateries, and are the Venetian equivalent of tapas—irresistible little snacks of every imaginable configuration. Eat them on sticks at the bar with an *ombra* as an *aperitif*, or at a table on a plate for lunch.

Like all finger food, *cicchetti* are devilishly addictive and I would defy anyone to stop at just one. The variety is overwhelming: *polpettine* (fried balls made with fish, meat, and vegetables); seafood and offal skewers; breads, toasts, and *polenta* bases; sardines, eggs, squid, and *charcuterie*. There truly isn't anything you can't make into a *cicchetto*.

How this book works

To reflect the fact that *cicchetti* are uniquely Venetian, each chapter is named for a special culinary aspect of the city. The chapter on fish and seafood recipes is named after the fish market, *La Pescheria*. The chapter on *crudo* is named after the fishing boats on which it was first made, *Il Peschereccio*. The chapter on cheese, eggs, and cured meats is named for the traditional delicatessen, *La Drogheria*. The vegetable chapter is called *L'Erbaria* after the Rialto fruit and vegetable markets. The meat recipes reside in a chapter called *La Beccheria*, or butcher. And finally, the drinks chapter is called *Il Bàcaro* after the Venetian wine bar. After that, there are chapters for the other regions of Italy that offer similar, sumptuous finger food.

The Venetian *cicchetto* differs from the *stuzzichino* in as much as a *cicchetto* would never be served alone but as part of a selection. Some, such as the *tartine* (small open-faced sandwich) and *polpettine* (fried ball or patty), are finger food, but others (such as the *seppie in umido* and *luganera*) are more like miniature *antipasti*. The *stuzzichino* is more of a serve-alone snack, as many are robust and very filling.

Both the *cicchetto* and *stuzzichino* reflect the cuisine of the area they come from in miniature, using typical ingredients, products, and the culinary traditions of the region. The Jewish tradition of deep-frying food is evident in the making of *polpettine*, as are the *frittata* (similar to an omlette) and the *torta*, marinated anchovies, and deep-fried small-fry.

I love cooking for friends but I do not want to spend all day preparing and then cooking the dishes when friends arrive. So I do as the Venetians do, and make a small selection of *cicchetti* to share as a meal with friends, and include good bread, *crostini*, and *polenta*. *Seppie in umido* or *luganera* can be made in advance and simply reheated. A *gratin* of scallops or *peoci* (mussels) can be popped in the oven at the last minute, along with a *polpettina* of fish, meat, or vegetables, and perhaps simple hard-boiled egg halves—*i mesi uovi*. The meal is then finished with a selection of cheeses and some fruit.

Of course, there is no reason why you should not just choose one of the *cicchetti* recipes and serve it as a starter or main course. I have taken a little license with the *cicchetti*, including *risi e bisi*, a Venetian *risotto* rather than a *cicchetto*. The *fagottini*, stuffed pasta bundles, are also perhaps more pasta than *cicchetti* but both are uniquely Venetian and deserve to take a bow in a book of sharing food. The meat and fish *carpaccio* dishes are not really *cicchetti* but invigorating Venetian starters.

Many of Valentina's *stuzzichini* can double as starters as well as being served on their own as light lunches with salads and snacks. *La focaccia al formaggio*, the *torta salata*, and the *frittatine* from Liguria are all delicious lunchtime treats, whereas tasty little morsels such as *sciatt* (cheese fritters from Bergamo) and liver *crostini* from Venice Giulia make perfect *canapés*.

Both Valentina and I have animated our recipes with stories and traditions associated with the food and I hope you will take time to read what we have written before taking to the kitchen to produce your own. The Venetian cook has much to teach us.

Most importantly, the Venetian cook wastes nothing. And the Venetian, by tradition, eats every part of the animal. You can't miss *fegato alla Veneziana*, calves' liver and onions, which is on the menu of just about every simple *osteria* and features in *cicchetti* too. *Nervetti*, *trippa*, and *spiensa*, nerves, tripe, and spleen (say them quickly and don't think about it), are among the stranger, and to our modern tastes less-palatable, toppings. Don't let this put you off, though. Venetians do eat a lot of curious things. Alongside the soused sardines on white *polenta*, tender artichokes, plump peppers, shrimp from the Venetian Laguna, tiny crisp fishcakes, fried squid, grilled octopus, and *crostini* with creamed salt cod, there is some serious offal eating to be done. If you find these classics on the menu you will know you have found an authentic Venetian *cicchetto* heaven.

There are eateries called *cicchetterie* that serve little besides *cicchetti*, and like other places serving *cicchetti*, they have a board hanging outside listing the offerings of the day in Venetian dialect. Common inclusions are hard-boiled egg halves served simply with salt, pepper, and a touch of Garda extra virgin olive oil; tiny octopi in various sauces; baby cuttlefish fried or roasted; deep-fried soft-shell crabs; grilled stuffed mussels; and *gratin* of scallops.

Salt cod is another favorite ingredient in the Venetian kitchen, and the inimitable *baccala' mantecata*, a concoction similar to the French *brandade*, is very popular. Served either as *crostini* or in little dishes, it is one of the crowning glories of any self-respecting *cicchetteria*. *Il bacala' alla giudia*, deep-fried fillets of salt cod, has all but disappeared from Venice, but you will find the recipe here.

Finally, there are the diminutive, melt-in-the-mouth, light-as-air *polpettine*. Made with fresh or leftover cooked fish, meat, and vegetables, *polpettine* are bolstered with bread or potatoes, moistened with milk, seasoned, coated in bread crumbs, and deep-fried.

The bàcaro

The *bàcaro* is unique to Venice. It is a traditional wine bar that has recently been reinvented as a kind of shabby-chic pub. Around the Rialto markets some of the *bàcari* are little more than a hole in the wall in a desirable location that dispenses wine, *aperitivi*, and *cicchetti*. On a typical Saturday lunchtime, bright young Venetians on their way home from shopping spill out onto the pavements quaffing their amber-colored Aperols and crimson Campari spritzers.

Even high water does little to deter this lunchtime ritual. The elegantly clad Venetian simply dons a pair of rubber boots or waders (never have waders been taken to such sartorial heights) to complete his understated designer outfit, rolls up a copy of the *Gazzetino*—the Venetian daily paper—and slides it into the back pocket of his jeans before striding out across the boardwalks toward the object of his hunger.

Venice's culinary observances also take place in the evening before going home for dinner. There are plenty of places in the *Erbaria* (the Rialto markets) alone: *L'Osteria al Pesador*, *Naranzaria*, *Banco Giro*, *Al Marca'*, and *Il Muro*. *Santa Margarita* is another lively area full of bars and *bàcari*.

Cicchetto and stuzzichino

Cicchetti are unique to Venice; you won't even find them elsewhere in the Veneto region, let alone in the other parts of Italy. This said, some *cicchetti*, such as marinated anchovies, have close relations across the family of Italian regions, but others, such as *sarde in saòr* (soused sardines) and *fegato alla Veneziana* (chopped liver *crostini*), are Venetian only-children.

    Cicchetti are more akin to Spanish *tapas* and Middle Eastern *mezze* than Italian *stuzzichini*, or snacks. It does not matter if you go to a bar, a *cicchetteria*, or a *bàcaro* (the shabby-chic Venetian wine bar), there will be lots to choose from. What's more, the Venetian expects to enjoy an array of *cicchetti* with his *aperitivo* at any time of the day. He may choose just one or two to stimulate the appetite or he may order a whole plateful. This is the norm in Venice; elsewhere in Italy you are more likely to be served just a few olives with a drink.

10 popular cicchetti

Seppie alla Veneziana—Black cuttlefish stew with *polenta*

Baccala' mantecata—Salt cod Venetian style

Le capesante gratinate—Scallop *gratin*

Le moeche—Soft-shell lagoon crabs

Trota affumicata con la mostarda Veneta—Hot-smoked trout and Venetian mustard

I mesi uovi—Hard-boiled egg halves

Sopressa con radicchio—*Sopressa*-wrapped radicchio

Crostini di fegato alla Veneziana—Venetian chopped liver *crostini*

Polpettine con manzo crudo—Beef patties

Carciofi violetti di S. Erasmo in padella—Sautéed Venetian purple-heart artichokes

In some regions, such as Liguria and Apulia, you will be offered marvelous fish, vegetable, and *charcuterie antipasti* as starters. Many of these will be similar to certain *cicchetti* but are served as part of a meal, not as snacks. Valentina will lead you on a culinary tour of the other Italian regions, where you will discover these delicious light bites, such as *mozzarella in carozza*, *suppli' di riso*, and *pannelle* (fritters). These are prepared by vendors in mobile stalls, street carts and lock-ups as street food snacks, while bars and *tavola caldas* sell them as substantial one-off snacks.

    Valentina's journey around the regions will introduce you to some of the finest *stuzzichini*—specialties created by Sicilian *friggitori* and *foccacceria*, Florentine *lampredottai*, Roman *rosticcerie*, snack bars, and stalls from Milan to Marsala. She has also written about the regions themselves, painting an unforgettable picture of their culinary and geographical treasures.

Overleaf: Palazzo Cavalli-Franchetti on the Grand Canal, with Santa Maria della Salute in the distance

Covering the basics

Butter or olive oil for sautéing and frying?

The Veneto region has the best of both worlds when it comes to natural oils and fats. It has a rich dairy industry that produces fine cheese, butter, and milk. It also has a microclimate around Lake Garda that produces the most wonderful extra virgin olive oil. If you are intolerant to dairy products you will still achieve good (if not quite as rich) results by using extra virgin olive oil with these recipes. Sunflower oil also produces light, crisp results and is not expensive.

Deep-frying

Many *cicchetti* are deep fried, but it is not essential to use a deep-fat fryer. A wok or large frying pan can be used, but clean oil is essential. After frying, leave the pan of oil to cool. Any debris will sink to the bottom of the pan and you can pour the cooled oil through a sieve into a jug, and then discard the debris from the bottom of the pan. This clean oil can be funneled back into the bottle it came from. You can use this oil two, three, or even four times so long as it smells and looks fresh, although you may want to add some fresh oil each time you use it. Old, stale, discolored oil makes food taste unpleasant, and is hard to digest. It gives fried food a bad name and a worse smell so do not overuse oil.

Heat the oil until it is bubbling hot to get the best results. To test its readiness, drop a piece of bread crust into the oil and if it starts to bubble and brown immediately, it is ready for frying. Work quickly, frying the food in batches. Never leave oil unattended for even a minute, and switch off the heat as soon as you have finished. Keep the pan of hot oil out of harm's way, and keep small children out of the kitchen while deep-frying.

Many people ask if they can shallow fry instead. It just does not work; deep-frying produces a crisp finish that shallow frying just can't do.

Have plenty of paper towels on hand to drain food as soon as it comes out of the hot fat.

Fried food needs to be served freshly cooked—there is no way around this—you have to stand, fry, and deliver!

When you have finished frying remember to switch off the heat. Burning oil is a common cause of house fires and it does untold damage.

Lard

When every household kept a pig, lard was the fat of choice for frying, deep-frying, and pastry making. For the past half-century we have turned to vegetable oils and fats for health reasons. Of late, there has been reevaluation on this thinking and it seems that pork fat is not so incredibly bad for us, as we have been led to think.

The fat in lard consists mostly of monounsaturated fatty acids (39 percent saturated fat, 11 percent polyunsaturated, and 45 percent monounsaturated) as compared to butter (50 percent saturated fat, four percent polyunsaturated, and 30 percent monounsaturated).

Statistics aside, good lard comes from good pigs, so make your own or buy it from your local butcher. I am not suggesting we go back to using lard for everything, but I am suggesting we stop avoiding it like the plague. Believe me, you won't be sorry. Frying in lard imparts a crisp texture but no flavor, so your *cicchetti* will just taste of honest ingredients. Frying in lard leaves no unpleasant frying smells in the kitchen either.

As you would with vegetable oil, you must pour off and filter the lard after each use and keep it in the fridge. You can use it two, three, or even four times. Discard when the lard discolors.

Polenta

Polenta is traditionally made in a copper *paiolo* with either yellow or white *polenta*—flour made from maize or corn. The flour is lightly sprinkled over simmering water and stirred and stirred, first with a metal whisk and then with the special *bastone* for about 45 minutes. It is always stirred in the same direction. The cooked *polenta* is then turned out on a board and cut with a wire into thick slices that are served with rich sauces or made into *pasticci*. Alternatively, cut *polenta* into small, thin slices and brown on a griddle to make bases for *cicchetti*.

Naturally, in a region where corn is a staple there are many variations on the theme from area to area within the Veneto. Near Asiago the *polenta* flour is cooked in milk, then potato purée, sautéed onion, and butter are added. In other areas potatoes are cooked until they start to disintegrate, then the *polenta* flour is added and stirred for an hour. Cook mushrooms until tender, then add the water and the *polenta* flour to make mushroom *polenta*. Make a thick bean purée, then add the water and then drizzle the *polenta* flour over the top. There are versions that stir in chopped dried fruit such as figs, and a simple variation that stirs in finely chopped fresh herbs, which makes for a fragrant *polenta*.

Soft polenta (*polenta morbida*)

Soft *polenta* served in terra-cotta dishes or in a pool on the plate has become a popular variation. Simply add a little extra hot water halfway through the stirring time. You can also experiment by adding warm cream or milk.

Instant polenta

If all that stirring is not for you, buy Italian-brand instant *polenta*. The method is the same but the stirring time is considerably shorter—it takes three to five minutes. I have really enjoyed using an instant *polenta* recently. Made by Alimenti Dallari, it is available from good delicatessens. For soft *polenta*, simply add extra hot water after a minute or so of stirring.

Block polenta

You can buy blocks of prepared *polenta*, which only need slicing, but the texture is very smooth, unlike real *polenta*, which has a grainy texture. I have used it but I don't recommend it.

Basic polenta recipe

4½ cups water

2¾ cups yellow or white polenta flour

1 tsp salt

Put the salted water in a large pan, copper if possible, and bring to a boil. Reduce the heat to a simmer and then drizzle the *polenta* from a great height into the simmering water. Using a metal balloon whisk, stir the *polenta* in a circular motion. Always stir in the same direction. Once the *polenta* is smooth use a *polenta* stick—a Scottish porridge stirrer (spirtle) would be perfect—otherwise use a wooden spoon and stir the *polenta* for 45 minutes.

Turn out onto a board and use a *polenta* wire or long-bladed knife to cut into slices half- to three-quarters of an inch thick.

Polenta bases for *cicchetti* using instant polenta

1¼ cups instant polenta flour

2 tsp chopped rosemary or other fresh herb (optional)

Prepare the *polenta* according to the instructions on the packet, adding the chopped rosemary if using. Pour into a small, rectangular, well-greased baking tray. Leave to cool, turn out onto a board, and cut into approximately 24 thin slices just less than half of an inch thick. Trim the slices to approximately half-an-inch by an inch-and-a-half and arrange on a baking tray. Brush lightly with oil and bake at 400°F for 10 minutes to warm through and lightly crisp edges. Alternatively, brown under a grill or on a griddle. Any leftover *polenta* can be wrapped and kept in the refrigerator for another day.

Deep-fried polenta

Leftover *polenta* can be wrapped in plastic wrap and kept in the fridge for another day. Cut the *polenta* into slices and fry. Then slit open and spread with cream cheese.

Tartine, crostini, and crostoni

Tartine

The Venetian *cicchetto* is often served on *tartine* or, as we would say, a bread and butter base for *cicchetto*. Use either thinly sliced (less than one-third of an inch) *ciabatta, filone,* or *baguette* and spread generously with butter. Top with the *cicchetto* of you choice.

Crostini

1 stale baguette or
   filone for 30-plus
   crostini
olive oil
2–3 garlic cloves,
   cut in half
   widthwise

This is a simple way of making *crostini* toasts, another base for *cicchetto*. It is important to use stale bread rather than fresh as it is much easier to cut. *Crostini* keep for weeks in an airtight container—always on hand for the unexpected guest.

Cut the *baguette* into diagonal slices one-third of an inch thick, arrange on a baking tray, and paint with olive oil. Cook in a hot oven, 400°F and bake until golden for about 10 to 15 minutes. Turn and return to the oven to brown for about five minutes more. Rub the hot *crostini* with cut garlic cloves and leave to cool on a rack.

If not using immediately, store in an airtight container until required.

Crostoni

1 small filone or
   ciabatta loaf
butter or extra virgin
   olive oil
1 garlic clove, halved

This is often used as the base for an open-face sandwich. Cut the bread into slices one-third of an inch thick, either spread with butter or brush with oil, and arrange on a baking tray. Cook in a hot oven at 400°F until crisp, about 20 minutes. Rub with the garlic clove. Perfect topped with wild mushrooms.

Buon appetito!

A Venetian perspective

Like many Venetians, Antonella Tagliapietra, who helped us with the styling of many of the dishes in this book, learned the basics of Italian cooking from her mother as a child. Only later would she come to realize just how strong the ties between food, family, and society are to her fellow Italians. Enjoying *cicchetti* is one way of renewing those bonds on a regular basis, although Antonella is hard-pressed to sum up the definitive dish. "Meatballs are very, very popular. They come in all sorts: meat, fish, eggplant."

"It's a habit that we have in Venice—a little nibble while we have a drink," Antonella explains. "We like drinking, and there is a large variety of wines. We like to meet up in bars to chat and have a drink." Socializing in this way is about having a good time, catching up with friends, and telling stories. "We don't like to get drunk, or to drink without eating. That's probably the real reason why we eat *cicchetti*."

Despite its growing prominence outside Italy, the culture of *cicchetti* is under threat in Venice from fast food chains and large grocery stores. Ingredients that were once seasonal and sold in the markets are available year-round in the bigger stores, at the expense of taste and flavor. Antonella insists that quality ingredients are worth the wait, and each season produces its own special harvest. "It's wonderful to see the seasons pass by and connect with them through cooking. In the autumn you can't find asparagus, but chestnuts are in season and there is plenty of pumpkin." The best *bàcari* continue to work with seasonal produce, grown by local farmers.

Antonella's love of Venetian food led her to found a cooking school, Arte Culinaria, eight years ago. It offers tutorials on traditional Venetian *antipasti*, pastas, *risottos*, *crespelle* (stuffed pancakes), and other dishes. She believes that enthusiasm for cooking often leads to a love of eating and sharing the experience with family and friends—a tradition common throughout Italy and much-envied elsewhere. Her students often form friendships while they are together. "It's like being in a family. We sit together at the table and eat what we produce." When the students sit down at the table with a glass of *prosecco* or local a wine to hand, there is a sense that *cicchetti* is doing its job—bringing people together.

Arte Culinaria, Via dall'Oglio 10, Cison di Valmarino, 31030 TV, Italy. For more information visit www.arteculinaria.it.

Pescheria

VENICE: SEAFOOD

I love the stillness and muted colors of Venice in the early morning, as it slowly and surely comes to life. The *traghetti* chug purposefully about their business of ferrying passengers to work and children to school. Barges stacked with rubble, building materials, merchandise, produce, and fish glide silently across the lagoon before being funneled into a canal and drawn along a quayside to unload.

A visit to the fish market, *la pescheria*, is fascinating. But to arrive at dawn, when everyone else is asleep and the barges are mooring and unloading along the broad quays of the Grand Canal, seems like a timeless dream.

The fish market hall is a colorful, porticoed, gothic construction hung with heavy canvas blinds, which are hauled up or dropped as needed. The fish are brought down from Tronchetto, the wholesale market, by barge to the market where dry-land and water-borne Venice converge. There are plans afoot to move the wholesale market way beyond the modern city confines to a (supposedly) more convenient location, but such a move might trigger the death of a city that has grown around its markets.

Today there are still 15 or so stalls, each competing for the business of the city's restaurants, its visitors, and the ever-declining number of locals still living in the heart of Venice. Though the number of vendors is dwindling, those that remain keep their high standards, competitive spirit, and their piercing alive-alive-o cries.

Polpettine di tonno fresco con acciughe e limone

Fresh tuna balls with anchovy and lemon

makes 30

8 oz fresh tuna,
 finely chopped

3 anchovy fillets,
 finely chopped

½ tbsp chopped
 capers

1 tbsp finely chopped
 flat-leaf parsley

⅓ cup fresh bread
 crumbs

juice and zest of 1
 lemon

1 pinch of chili flakes

½ egg

salt and black pepper

lemon wedges,
 to serve

Polpettine are the trademark *cicchetto* of the fashionable *bàcaro*. They come in many guises—meat, fish, and vegetable—and were originally made to use up leftovers. There are many versions of the basic recipe. Some use bread soaked in milk, others use bread crumbs, and some use potato; it's simply a question of what you have available. Flavorings are varied too; this recipe uses capers and anchovies to enhance the tuna.

These are the quantities to make a large amount of *polpettine* but if you just want to make a few with some leftover tuna you will be walking in the footsteps of the thrifty Venetian cook.

Mix the tuna, anchovies, capers, and parsley with the bread crumbs and lemon zest and juice. Add the chili, half an egg, salt, and pepper to taste.

Crack open the egg into a large bowl and whisk lightly with a fork. Put the flour in a second bowl and the bread crumbs in a third bowl.

Roll teaspoons of the mixture into balls, dust them in flour, dip in the egg and lastly roll in the bread crumbs. Put on a tray and put in the fridge until required.

Heat a wok or large, heavy-based pan containing the oil. When it starts to smoke, drop a crust of bread in. If the oil starts to froth around the bread and the bread turns golden, it is ready and you can start frying the *polpettine* in batches.

Do not overcrowd the pan—fry maybe six or eight at a time and transfer with a slotted spoon to paper towels to drain, then put on a serving plate in a warm oven until the others are ready.

These are best served straight from the pan but you can serve them cold or reheat in a hot oven.

Serve with lemon wedges.

To fry

1 egg

½ cup all-purpose
 flour

1 cup dried bread
 crumbs

4 cups sunflower oil
 or lard, for frying

Polpettine di granchio al timo

Crab meat and thyme balls

makes 30

½ lb cooked brown
    crab meat

2 slices of bread,
    soaked in milk and
    squeezed dry

2 tbsp chopped
    flat-leaf parsley

1 tsp fresh thyme

finely grated zest of
    1 lemon

pinch of chili flakes

½ egg, to bind

salt

1 lemon, cut into
    wedges for serving

To fry

1 egg, beaten

1 oz all-purpose flour

1 cup dried bread
    crumbs

4 cups sunflower oil
    or lard

This *cicchetto* is entirely my own invention. It is very much in the style and spirit of the Venetian *cicchetto* and I would be very surprised if some *bàcaro* somewhere does not make *polpettine* using brown crab meat. I have used one of my favorite combinations of flavors: brown crab meat, fresh thyme, and chili.

Put the crab meat in a bowl and mash with a fork to eliminate lumps. Add the prepared bread and mash vigorously to make a smooth mixture. Add the herbs, lemon zest, chili, half an egg, and mix well, adding salt if necessary. The mixture should be fairly wet.

Crack the egg into a large bowl and whisk lightly. Put the flour in another large bowl and the bread crumbs in a third bowl.

Roll teaspoons of the mixture into balls, dust them in flour, dip in the egg, and then roll in the bread crumbs. Place on a tray in the refrigerator until required.

Heat a wok or large, heavy frying pan containing the oil. When it starts to smoke, drop a crust of bread in. If the oil starts to froth around the bread and turn golden, it is ready and you can start frying the *polpettine* in batches.

Do not overcrowd the pan—fry maybe six or eight at a time and transfer with a slotted spoon to paper towels to drain, then put on a serving plate in a warm oven until the others are ready.

These are best served straight from the pan but you can serve them cold or reheat in a hot oven.

Serve with lemon wedges.

Seppie alla Veneziana

Black cuttlefish stew with polenta

serves 4

1 lb cuttlefish or
    squid

extra virgin olive oil

1 very small onion,
    finely chopped

3 garlic cloves, finely
    chopped

1 bunch of flat-leaf
    parsley, chopped

1 glass of soave delle
    Venezie white wine

2 tsp cuttlefish ink

1 tbsp tomato paste

¾ cup fish stock

1 cup freshly made
    polenta (see page 16)

salt and black pepper

This inky black sauce always makes me think of canal waters at night in Venice, lapping around the moored gondolas and reflecting the oily lamp light.

The dish is one of my favorite Venetian dishes, served either with *polenta*, *bigoli* (as the Venetians call *spaghetti*), or *risotto*. I used to make it regularly when I could buy the cuttlefish with black ink sacs still attached but now it is a thing of the past. You can buy neat little packets of dried *nero di seppie* (cuttlefish ink), which is a great substitute.

Clean the cuttlefish carefully, removing and reserving the pouch containing the ink. Cut away the beak and eyes . Pull the head and tentacles away from the body, and the insides will come away attached to the head. Cut them off and discard. Pull away any remaining detritus from the sac, rinse, and pat dry. Cut the tentacles and body into small pieces and wrap in a cloth to dry.

Pour two tablespoons of extra virgin olive oil into a saucepan over medium heat. Add the onion and garlic and sweat gently until tender. Add the prepared cuttlefish or squid and the flat-leaf parsley and cook for five minutes. Increase the heat and add the wine and cook for a further two minutes or until evaporated, then add the squid ink if using. The more ink you add, the blacker the dish. Dilute the tomato paste with three tablespoons of stock, stir in, and season to taste.

Reduce the heat to very low, cover the pan, and simmer for 30 minutes or until tender, adding a little more stock if the frying pan dries out too much. Ideally leave to stand for 12 to 24 hours before serving.

Serve over individual helpings of *polenta*.

Aringa affumicata con la senape

Kipper fillets in mustard and lemon sauce

makes 18

6 trimmed kipper
   fillets

6 tbsp mild
   mustard

3 tbsp mayonnaise
   or cream

juice of 2 lemons

1 heaped tbsp finely
   chopped cocktail
   pickles

1 heaped tbsp finely
   chopped capers

There are certain culinary traditions in the region of the Veneto that remind us of the proximity of Austria, and the use of mustard-laden dressings for cured fish is certainly one of them. Some of them are very strong and I have adapted them by adding a little mayonnaise to soften the flavor. Mustard lovers may prefer to leave it out. The mustard also prolongs the shelf life of the kipper.

Check the kipper fillets for bones by running your fingers lightly along the flesh. If using whole kippers, open them up, separate the fillets with a sharp knife, cut a V down the center of the fillets, and trim the edges. Cut each kipper fillet diagonally (along the natural flake line of the fish) into three equal-sized pieces, and arrange on a large platter.

   Mix all the other ingredients in a small bowl and pour over the kipper pieces. Cover with plastic wrap and, if time allows, leave to stand in the fridge for several hours or overnight.

Baccala' mantecato

Salt cod Venetian-style

serves 6 to 8
makes 36 to 40

1 lb 8 oz salt cod

1 small onion

1 small carrot

1 celery stalk

large bunch of
flat-leaf parsley,
finely chopped
(reserve the stalks)

1 bay leaf

1 sprig of thyme

1 tsp black
peppercorns

½ cup extra virgin
olive oil

1 garlic clove, finely
chopped

To serve

1 baguette or 8 oz
freshly made
polenta (see page 16)

lemon wedges
(optional)

In days gone by salt cod was the mainstay of every sea-faring nation, and Venice was no exception. However, rather than calling it stock fish, as it is known elsewhere in Italy, in Venice it was and is known as *baccala'*. *Baccala'* is the word that the Italians normally use for fresh cod. Every city across the region has its specialty dish, and Venice is famous for *baccala' mantecato*, which is very similar to the French *brandade* and is probably one of the most well-known *cicchetti*.

Just like *polenta* and *risotto*, *baccala' mantecato* takes a lot of stirring; goodness knows how arm-breaking it must have been in the days before food processors. It takes a long time with the food processor but do not give up on it; it is well worth the effort.

Some recipes cook the *baccala'* in milk, which creates a creamier, but I feel less flavorful, concoction.

The day before making this recipe, soak the salt cod in cold water for 24 hours, changing the water three or four times.

Rinse the fish and pat it dry then transfer to a large frying pan. Add the onion, carrot, celery, parsley stalks, bay leaf, thyme, and peppercorns and cover with water. Bring gently to simmering point and cook over low heat until the fish flakes easily, say 30 to 45 minutes. This will vary according to the quality and type of salt cod used.

Drain the cod but reserve the cooking liquid. Discard the vegetables and transfer the salt cod to a food processor fitted with a plastic blade. Start working the salt cod, adding a ladle of the cooking water. When the cod begins to look creamy start adding the extra virgin olive oil in a gentle stream. When this has been incorporated, add the chopped garlic and flat-leaf parsley. If the mixture is very solid it may be necessary to add an extra ladle of cooking liquid to slacken it. It should be soft and fluffy.

Transfer to a serving dish and spread on slices of crusty bread or toasted *polenta*. Serve with lemon wedges.

Gratinata di peoci

Gratin of mussels

makes 25 to 50

1 lb mussels

generous ½ cup of
fresh bread crumbs

1 fat garlic clove,
finely chopped

1 handful of flat-
leaf parsley, finely
chopped

1 tomato, cut in half,
deseeded, drained,
and cut into tiny dice

salt and black pepper

extra virgin olive oi

This simple *gratin* of mussels recipe can be adapted to make *gratin* of scallops, clams, or razor fish. They are delicious warm or cold and of course the shell provides the perfect finger food container. In this recipe the *gratin* is made with fresh white bread crumbs flavored with tomato, garlic, and flat-leaf parsley but when fresh tomatoes are out of season, leave them out.

Preheat the oven to 350°F. Clean the mussels in running cold water. Scrub the shells, scrape off any barnacles, and pull away the beard (the filament that hangs out of the shell). Leave to stand in cold water, and when all are clean, drain in a colander.

Open the mussel shells by sliding a short-bladed knife carefully between the two shells and turning gently to prize the shells apart. As you open them, carefully drain the juice into a bowl. Discard the empty half-shells and arrange the half-shells containing the mussels on an oiled baking tray. If the mussels are small and do not fill the shells completely, put two mussels in each shell.

Put the bread crumbs into the bowl of mussel juice, and add the garlic, parsley, tomato, and salt and pepper to taste. Mix lightly and fill the shells with the mixture. Drizzle the mussels with oil and bake for 15 minutes or until golden.

Ostriche fritte

Deep-fried oysters

makes 24

24 fresh oysters

3 tbsp all-purpose
flour

salt and black pepper

2 small eggs

4 cups sunflower
oil, for frying

lemon wedges, to
serve

There is nothing that can compare with a fresh, raw oyster, but for those people who just don't fancy uncooked shellfish, this is the next best way of eating them. They are fried quickly in oil with just a veiling of flour and a light seasoning of salt and pepper.

Scrub the oyster shells , put them in a large pot, and cover with a lid. Put the pan on high heat and shake the pan until the shells open. Switch off the heat and leave the pot to cool on the side. Strain any juices from the pan and reserve, then scoop out the oysters when they are cool enough to handle.

Put the flour in a large bowl and season with salt and pepper.

Beat the eggs in a bowl and add the oyster juices.

Dust the oysters in flour, then drop the oysters in the egg mixture, then toss in the flour again.

Heat the oil in a wok or large, heavy frying pan. When it starts to smoke, drop a crust of bread in. If the oil starts to froth around the bread and the bread turns golden, it is ready and you can start frying the oysters in batches.

Do not overcrowd the pan; fry six or eight at a time and transfer to paper towels to drain. Put the oysters on a serving plate in a warm oven until all are ready. Serve straight away with lemon wedges.

Filetti di baccala' fritti "alla Giudia"

Jewish-style salt cod fritters

makes 16

1 lb salt cod

4 oz oo flour

salt

¼ cup warm water

½ tsp dry yeast

1 tbsp butter, melted

4¼ cups sunflower oil, for frying

Baccala' features in regional dishes right across the Veneto region. There was a time when these fried fillets of salt cod were as popular as *baccala' mantecato* but they have all but disappeared from the modern *cicchetti* menu. This recipe comes from the traditional Jewish cooking in the ghetto. Note that these can be very salty if the fish is not soaked for the alotted time first, and that you will need oo flour.

Soak the cod for 48 hours in cold water, changing the water three or four times. You can make the fritters with the thickest part of the fish, cut from the center of the fillet, and use the trimmings to make *baccala' mantecata* (see page 27).

Cut the thick part of the fillet into three-quarter-inch wide slices.

Put the flour into a bowl, and add a pinch of salt, the water, and the yeast. Mix well. Add the melted butter and mix again. Leave the batter to rest for three hours at room temperature before using it.

Heat a wok or large, heavy frying pan contaiing the oil. When it starts to smoke, drop a crust of bread in. If the oil froths around the bread and the bread turns golden, it is ready and you can start frying the *baccala'* in batches.

Do not overcrowd the pan; fry two or three at a time and transfer with a slotted spoon to paper towels to drain. Put them on a serving plate in a warm oven until the others are ready.

It may be necessary to adjust the temperature of the oil while frying, as it can overheat and brown the fish too quickly.

Sprinkle with salt and serve at once.

Sarde in saòr Venete

Soused sardines

serves 4

4 cups sunflower
oil or 1 lb lard

2 small onions,
finely sliced

½ cup good white
wine vinegar

1 lb fresh sardines

2 tbsp all-purpose
flour

salt and black pepper

2 tbsp golden raisins,
soaked in hot water
for 5 minutes and
squeezed dry

1 tbsp pine nuts

It is traditional in Venice to eat *sarde in saòr* on the *Festa del Renditore* on the third Sunday in July, but the dish appears on *cicchetti* menus whenever sardines are plentiful. The recipe was first developed by seafarers who, having to stay at sea for long periods of time, learned to prepare fish so that it would keep longer. The sardines are fried in lard and then layered in white wine vinegar with some finely sliced onions, lemon zest, golden raisins, and pine nuts. The addition of onion would have helped combat scurvy.

Cover the base of a frying pan with a little oil, put over low heat, and fry the onions until transparent and tender, taking care not to brown them. Add a tablespoon of cold water from time to time to keep the onions from browning.

Transfer to a shallow dish, add the vinegar, and leave until quite cold. Scale the sardines and pull off their heads (the intestines should come away at the same time). Cut open along the belly and scrape out any remaining intestines, then rinse under the cold tap and pat dry.

Open the sardines like a book and turn over; press down hard with the flat of your hand; and then turn the sardine back over. Pull out the backbone, which should come away easily.

Close the sardines up and lightly dust in seasoned flour, shaking off the excess. Pour two inches of sunflower oil into a frying pan (or one pound of lard in a deep pan) and set over high heat. When bubbling hot, add the sardines one at a time and fry in batches until golden, transfer to paper towels to drain, and then leave to cool.

Layer the sardines, onions, the soaked raisins, and the pine nuts in a shallow dish and leave for at least 24 to 48 hours in the refrigerator before serving.

Moeche al vino bianco

Soft-shell crabs cooked in white wine

makes 20

2 lbs 2 oz frozen soft-
shell crabs, thawed

1 cup all-purpose flour

5 tbsp butter

2 tbsp chopped
flat-leaf parsley

1 tsp dry white wine

salt and black pepper

Moeca is the Venetian dialectal word for soft-shell crab (*moeche*), a seasonal delicacy. Even though I have been a fairly regular visitor to Venice, years have gone by without seeing them on the menu, and it is exciting to be there when they make an appearance. It is possible to buy frozen soft-shell crabs outside of the Veneto and so I include the recipe here.

Toss the crabs in the flour. Put the butter in a large frying pan. When it starts to sizzle, add the crabs and fry, turning in the sizzling butter. Add the flat-leaf parsley, white wine, salt, and pepper. Cook for five to 10 minutes depending on size. Serve hot.

Left: Sarde in saòr Venete

Gamberetti di fiume con speck e lime

Speck with prawns and lime

Speck is a classic regional cure, and like other cured pork, it goes well with seafood. I lunched on these one day in a bar near the fish market and have been making my own version ever since. The Venetian ones were served on *tartine* (see page 17) but I like them on brown bread. I sometimes omit the bread entirely and simply roll the crayfish mixture in a slice of *speck*. Don't forget the lime zest garnish!

Put the mayonnaise and tomato paste in a bowl. Add the chili, lime juice, and zest and stir. Add the crayfish tails or shrimp and finely chopped celery and stir them into the sauce. Cover and set aside.

Cut the *speck* into 12 pieces with kitchen scissors. Put the *speck* pieces on the bread and spoon the crayfish or shrimp mixture on top. Top each with a couple of strands of lime zest, some celery leaves, and a hint of chili.

makes 12

The sauce

- 3 tbsp mayonnaise
- 2 tsp sun-dried tomato paste
- 1 pinch of chili powder
- 1 tsp of lime juice
- 1 tsp lime zest
- 4 oz crayfish tails or shrimp, peeled and cooked
- 1 stick of celery, finely chopped

To serve

- 3 oz speck or other cured ham, thinly sliced
- 3 thin slices brown bread, buttered and with crusts cut off
- ½ a lime, cut into julienne strips
- extra chili powder

Trota affumicata con mostarda

Hot-smoked trout and mustard bites

This is another combination of mustard and smoked fish. Make sure you cut everything very finely so that the dish looks refined. The bread should be only one-third of an inch thick. *Cicchetti* must look appetizing and dainty!

Combine the mustard, mayonnaise, lemon juice, gherkins, and candied fruits in a bowl. Add salt and pepper to taste and stir well.

Cut each fish fillet down the center and cut each fillet into five lozenge-shaped pieces. Cover each one with a spoonful of dressing, cover, and leave to stand for an hour or even overnight before serving. Transfer each covered fillet to the sliced bread or *crostini*. Arrange on a large plate and serve.

makes 20

- 2 level tbsp mild French mustard
- 2 generous tbsp mayonnaise
- juice of 1 lemon
- 9 tiny cocktail pickles, finely chopped
- 1 generous tbsp candied fruits, finely chopped

- salt and black pepper
- 2 hot smoked trout fillets, approx 7 oz
- 3 thin slices of brown bread, crusts cut off, and cut into 6 to 8 triangles, or 20 crostini (see page 17)

Right: Gamberetti di fiume con speck e lime

Le sepoine in umido con bastoncini di polenta

Baby squid or cuttlefish in a light tomato sauce with polenta sticks

serves 4 or makes 24 bites

1 lb baby squid or cuttlefish

extra virgin olive oil

1 small bunch of flat-leaf parsley, finely chopped, plus extra to serve

1–2 garlic cloves, finely chopped

½ glass of soave wine

1 ladleful of plain tomato sauce or 1 tbsp tomato paste dissolved in 1 tbsp water

polenta slices (see page 16) or crostini, to serve

In the fish market in Venice it is possible to buy cuttlefish and tiny tender squid no bigger than the end of your thumb; these require no cleaning but sadly you are unlikely to come across them outside Italy, or specifically the Laguna. However, elsewhere you can buy squid about three inches long that are almost as tender.

Clean the cuttlefish or squid, and pull the tentacles away from the sacs. Discard any matter that comes away with the tentacles, rinse out the sac, and pull out and discard the "plastic" blade inside. Cut the tentacles and sac into rings and dry thoroughly.

Put a medium-sized frying pan over high heat. When hot, add enough oil to cover the base and add the squid immediately. Stir-fry for a few minutes to remove any excess moisture, reduce the heat to medium, and add the flat-leaf parsley and garlic. Stir-fry for a few more minutes. Add the wine and stir to evaporate, then add the tomato sauce or paste. Cover and cook for 30 minutes over a low heat. As the pan dries out it may be necessary to add a little more sauce. Transfer to a dish and sprinkle with the finely chopped flat-leaf parsley.

Serve with slices of *polenta* or on *crostini*.

Le capesante gratinate

Scallop gratin

makes 6 large
or 18 queen
scallops

6 large scallops
and coral

3 tbsp fresh bread
crumbs

1 tbsp butter, melted

1 large garlic clove,
finely chopped

2–3 tbsp finely
chopped flat-leaf
parsley

salt and black pepper

extra virgin olive oil

6 large scallop shells
or 18 queen scallop
shells, to serve

The Venetian lagoon offers a precious catch of dainty queen scallops that are the perfect size for a *gratin* platter. I have rarely seen these little beauties for sale in their shells other than in Venice. I have therefore given quantities for large scallops. These days it is increasingly difficult to buy hand-dived scallops in their shells, so I keep a dozen or so scallop shells handy for just such a recipe.

If the scallops are still in their shells, prize open the shells with a short-bladed knife. Cut out the scallop, pulling away any membrane that surrounds it. Pull away the coral (the orange roe attached to it) and reserve. Pull away the foot of the scallop, pat the scallop dry, and arrange on paper towels. Scrub the dish-shaped scallop shell in soapy water, drain, dry, and reserve.

Mix the bread crumbs, butter, garlic, and parsley, and season to taste in a large bowl. Lightly oil the scallop shells and arrange on a baking tray. Dip the scallops and coral in the crumb mixture and transfer one to each shell. Drizzle with oil and bake at 400°F for 15 minutes or until the bread crumbs are crisp and golden.

Scatter any leftover crumb mixture over the scallop and the shells.

Canocce o scampi al prezzemolo

Fresh shrimp in parsley dressing

serves 6

2 lbs whole raw
jumbo shrimp

3 tbsp extra virgin
olive oil

2 tbsp finely chopped
flat-leaf parsley,

salt and black pepper

prosecco (optional),
to serve

If you have ever walked around the Pescheria, *il mercato al momento,* in Venice you will know what an amazing variety of shrimp are available, all sizes and colors, and so fresh. All are perfect for making *cicchetti*, and perfect for *crudo* too. It can be difficult to work out what to buy, but I like to go for something I have not seen or tried before. Back home, however, it is not easy to find raw, fresh shrimp of any sort and you may be forced into buying frozen ones, but this recipe will still be delicious.

Put a large pan of water on to boil with some salt. When the water comes to a boil, add the shrimp and cook for four to five minutes. Drain and pull off the shell, and discard. Arrange the shrimp in a shallow dish.

Mix the extra virgin olive oil, parsley, salt, and pepper to taste and pour over the shrimp. Serve with a glass of chilled *prosecco* if you like.

Crudo di branzino con agrumi

Citrus-marinated sea bass

serves 4

4 fresh sea bass fillets,
  frozen for 48 hours
  and defrosted
2 tsp grated
  fresh ginger
1 tsp salt crystals
1 orange
1 lemon
1 lime
olive oil

I remember eating the inspiration for this recipe at least a decade ago in Venice on a cold dark November night. We had been recommended the restaurant (I only wish I had kept a note of its name —I have never managed to find it again) and once there we ate from a stunningly creative menu. On my return home I did my own take on the sea bass starter which I have made in many guises since then.

Lay a sea bass fillet skin side down on a chopping board, tail towards you. Hold the tail and introduce the blade of a knife between the skin and the fish and carefully slide the knife along the skin close to the board, lift the fish away from the skin as you do so. Lay the fillets in a shallow dish in a single layer (skin side down) rub the grated ginger root over the fish, add the salt crystals crushing them between the fingers as you do so.

Cut the citrus zest into julienne and reserve. Squeeze the citrus juice over the fish, cover and put in the fridge for 2 hours.

After this time pour away the marinade and slice the fish fillets thinly and arrange the slices on 4 plates, top with the reserved zest and drizzle with oil.

Cape sante crude alla nettarina bianca

Nectarine-marinated scallops with lime

serves 4

2 white nectarines
juice of 1 lime
3 tbsp olive oil
2 pinches of salt
  crystals
1 tsp honey
1 pinch of chili flakes

12 large scallops,
  frozen for 48 hours
  and defrosted
rind of 1 lime, cut
  into julienne strips

I love the combination of lime juice, chili, and fish. Added to this the puréed pulp of white nectarine, it is the perfect combination of flavors to enhance silky fresh scallops and peeled prawns, not to mention monkfish and sea bass.

Lightly score the nectarines around the middle and immerse in boiling water for a few minutes to blanch. Lift the nectarines out of the water with a spoon and peel off the skin. Cut into quarters and discard the stone. Put the nectarines in a blender with the lime juice, oil, salt crystals, honey, and chili flakes. Reduce to a purée. Cut the scallops into paper-thin rounds and divide between four plates, arranged in rows. Pour the purée over the scallops and top with a few strips of lime rind. Leave to marinate in a cool place for an hour. Serve with crusty bread and butter.

Right: Crudo di branzino con agrumi

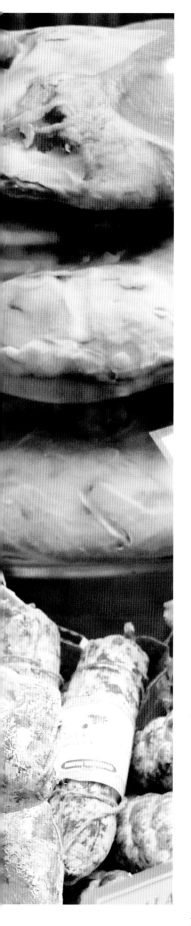

La Drogheria

VENICE: EGGS, CHEESE, CURED MEAT

The Venetian delicatessen is known as *la drogheria*; every *sestiere* (district) has one or two within the cluster of little shops that serve the community. The visitor would do well to search them out on a walk through the quiet alleyways, charming squares, and shady spaces not far from the grandiose St. Mark's Square, away from the hustle and bustle of tourist traps.

The Veneto region is immensely rich. It is home to Padua, Verona, Treviso, the Palladian Villas, Lake Garda, the Dolomite Mountains, and rich agricultural land. It boasts 370 traditional products including cheeses, wines, *charcuterie*, spirits, drinks, cured and fresh meats, fish, baked goods, and confectionery, and you will find most of these in a typical *drogheria*.

If you do not want to wander far, there are many good *drogheria* to be found in the streets around the Rialto markets. Cheeses such as *formaggio di morlacco* and *caciotte di asiago* are unique to the region and must be sampled when you are there. You may also discover that many of the popular cheeses are easy to find in your local deli, such as *gorgonzola*, *taleggio*, *grana padano*, and *ricotta*. There are hundreds of cured meats such as *lardo*, *l'ossocollo*, *speck*, and *soppressa* to enjoy. The kind of choice you find in the *drogheria* could inspire a thousand *cicchetti*.

Frittata di radicchio

Gardener's frittata

serves 4 or
makes 24 to
30 mini bites

5 heads of radicchio
or other seasonal
vegetables, sautéed

5 eggs

1½ oz grana padano,
grated

salt and black pepper

2 tbsp butter

3 tbsp extra virgin
olive oil

The Veneto is famous for its many radicchio varieties: *Treviso,
Verona, Castelfranco, rosa di Gorizia,* and so on.

A *frittata* is the most wonderful standby as it makes a
formidable lunch for the unexpected guest with a few eggs,
some grated cheese, and whatever vegetables you have on hand.
Add about one lightly sautéed, thinly sliced zucchini, mushrooms,
peppers, or eggplant cut into small cubes. It is also a great way to
use up cooked vegetables.

Serve with fried potatoes or crusty bread and salads for lunch
or simply cut into bite-sized squares to serve with drinks.

Cut the raw radicchio into slivers.

Beat the eggs well and stir in the grated *grana padano* and a generous
grinding of black pepper and a little salt. Mix in the radicchio and leave to stand
for five minutes.

Put the butter and oil in a fairly large, deep frying pan over medium heat.
When the butter has melted and the oil starts to bubble, add the egg and
radicchio mixture. When the egg mixture has set enough to be able to flip
over (this may take 20 minutes), tip the *frittata* upside down onto a large plate.
Carefully slide it back into the pan top-side down, then leave for 10 minutes
until the *frittata* is quite set and golden on top and bottom.

Turn out and serve hot or cold; cut like a cake to share and serve with salads.
Alternatively, cut into bite-sized pieces and arrange on a serving platter.

I mesi uovi

Hard-boiled egg halves

makes 12

6 eggs

6 anchovy fillets, plus
    extra to garnish

1 tbsp chopped flat-
    leaf parsley, plus
    extra to garnish

black pepper

No *cicchetti* spread would be complete without hard-boiled egg halves. These are generally served with a simple dressing of olive oil, salt, and pepper with perhaps the addition of a scrap of anchovy, making a simple and colorful dish for a *cicchetti* table.

Put the eggs in a small pan and cover with cold water. Put on medium to high heat and bring to a boil. Simmer for 10 minutes and then put the pan under running cold water. Drain, tap the eggs to crack the shell, and leave to cool.

Finely chop the anchovies and add the flat-leaf parsley and then work them to a paste with a mortar and pestle

When the eggs are quite cold, cut in half lengthwise. Turn the yolks out and add them, with a good grinding of pepper, to the anchovy and flat-leaf parsley paste, and mix until smooth.

Fill and mound up the egg-white cavity with the mixture, top each one with a small leaf of flat-leaf parsley or an anchovy roll, and arrange on a serving dish.

Le uova di quaglia e acciughe crostini fritti

Quail egg crostini

makes 12

sunflower oil

3 slices white bread,
    crusts cut off and
    cut into quarters

6 anchovy fillets,
    mashed

12 quail's eggs

When I was first approached to write a book on *cicchetti,* I went into a frenzy of recipe testing. I bought an array of suitable ingredients including a box of quails' eggs, which I could not resist frying along with little squares of bread. They looked and tasted splendid served alongside sardines, salt cod, scallops, and asparagus, and I felt they followed in the finest tradition of the *cicchetto.*

Heat a large frying pan. When hot add enough sunflower oil to cover the base. Add the prepared bread squares, fry until golden on both sides, and put onto paper towels to drain. Spread the fried bread with a little of the mashed anchovy, then transfer to a warm plate in the oven.

Carefully crack open the quail's eggs into a cup one at a time and fry the eggs until the whites are set. Put the egg on the fried bread and serve warm.

Variation:

Use grated *grana padano* or bits of *speck* instead of mashed anchovy to flavor the fried bread.

Left: I mesi uovi

Cicchetti con la ricotta e lardo

Ricotta and pancetta crostini

makes 24

8 oz ricotta

⅔ cup walnuts or hazelnuts, chopped

salt and black pepper

1 oz thinly sliced lardo or unsmoked pancetta, cut into 4-in lengths

24 crostini (see page 17)

The combination of *ricotta* with nuts and *lardo* is a traditional take on the Venetian *cicchetto* that I have enjoyed on many occasion while staying in the region. However, it is a combination difficult to replicate here as we do not have the equivalent of *lardo*.

You cannot translate the Italian word *lardo* with the English word lard. They are both products of the pig, but Italian *lardo* is cured pork back fat, and like *prosciutto* it is served sliced paper-thin as an *antipasto*. It is soft, tender, and full of flavor. Anglo-Saxon lard is the much-maligned rendered pork fat, used melted for frying or cold and hard for making pastry.

Lardo is a bit of a shock at first sight. We have become quite used to the proportion of fat to flesh of the average *prosciutto* or *pancetta* but not to a paper-thin slice of fat. One bite, however, is enough to persuade you otherwise.

Lardo is sometimes creamed with rosemary and spread between two magnificent slices of country bread to make a sandwich fit for a king.

I have used crispy *pancetta* to top the creamy *ricotta* mixture rather than the requisite *lardo*, but if you are making this recipe in the Veneto, please use simple paper-thin *lardo* and drink a glass of *amarone* with it. I look forward to the day when it is available overseas alongside so many other good ingredients that were once unheard of beyond Italy's borders.

Mix the *ricotta*, nuts, a little salt, and a good grinding of black pepper to taste.

Dry-fry the *pancetta* pieces to a crisp, drain on paper towels, and leave to cool. Spread the *ricotta* mixture on the *crostini* and top with strips of crisp *pancetta*. However, if you are lucky enough to have access to some *lardo*, simply top the *ricotta* with a looped, paper-thin slice.

Sopressa con radicchio

Sopressa-wrapped radicchio

**serves 4 or
makes 8**

4 heads of radicchio
or red chicory

2 tbsp butter

1 tbsp extra virgin
olive oil

salt and black pepper

3–4 tbsp red wine

8 thin slices of
sopressa salami or
other large salami

grilled polenta slices
(see page 16),
to serve

Sopressa is yet another specialty from beautiful Treviso in the Veneto region; it is a pale pink, soft, fresh-tasting, wide-girth *salami* made with 70 percent of the very best-quality lean pork mixed with 30 percent *pancetta* fat, salt, and spices, and matured in skins for six to eight months. There are many variations of the *sopressa*. Lean, cured pork fillet or strips of *pancetta*, *ossocollo*, *speck*, brawn, and other cured meats are buried in the center of the *sopressa* and then cured.

Clean and cut the radicchio in half lengthwise.

Put a large frying pan over medium heat, add the butter and olive oil, and when the butter has melted and begins to bubble, add the radicchio halves and fry until they start to wilt. Turn and fry on the other side, and add salt and pepper. Add the wine and cook until evaporated, turning the radicchio in the pan juices. Transfer to a serving plate cut side down, lay a slice of *sopressa* over each radicchio half, and serve hot on slices of grilled *polenta*.

Alternatively, lay the wrapped radicchio on thinly sliced *polenta* on a baking tray and leave to cool. When ready to serve, put in an oven preheated to 400°F for eight minutes or until bubbling hot.

Variation:

Serve the whites of leeks sautéed and prepared this way, or use *speck* instead of *sopressa*.

Polenta fritta con lo stracchino

Deep-fried polenta sticks filled with stracchino cheese

makes 12-plus

4 oz instant polenta

1 tbsp finely chopped
rosemary, sage,
thyme, marjoram,
or flat-leaf parsley
(optional)

4 cups sunflower oil

8 oz stracchino or
taleggio cheese

This again is one of those dishes that has been on the back-burner for years. To be honest, I never used to be a great *polenta* fan unless it came with a sausage casserole or something similarly rich and delicious. Either *polenta* has become more refined or my tastes have become more rustic, because I like it these days, especially when made with fresh herbs and left slightly creamy. However, back in the old days this recipe for fried *polenta* with *stracchino* was a favorite of mine.

Make the *polenta* according to the instructions on the packet, while mixing add the chopped herbs of choice, and then pour into a well-greased rectangular baking pan. Leave to cool, then turn out onto a board and cut into fingers measuring 1 x 1 x 3 inches.

Heat a wok or large, heavy-based pan containing the oil. When it starts to smoke, drop a crust of bread in. If the oil starts to froth around the bread and the bread turns golden, it is ready and you can start frying the *polenta* fingers in batches. Take care, as the water content of *polenta* is quite high and the oil can spit quite fiercely. When golden brown, drain the *polenta* on paper towels. Split open, spread *stracchino* in the middle, and serve at once.

L'Erbaria

VENICE: VEGETABLES

No visit to Venice is complete without a visit to the colorful fruit, vegetable, and fish markets where the seasons create an ever-changing kaleidoscope of delicious things to eat. Much of the beautiful, fresh produce is proudly labelled "Nostrano"—Our Own.

The markets are at the heart of Venice. The Erbaria and Naranzeria specialize in fruit and vegetables, once grown only on the islands of Sant'Erasmo and Vignole. The fish market was once exclusively stocked by the fishermen of the Laguna and surrounding sea.

The history of the Rialto markets goes hand-in-hand with the growth of Venice herself. The markets were established in the eleventh century around a crossing point where East met West. The trading of salt, sugar, pepper, and spices brought in the wealth of the Serenissima and provided the riches on which her empire grew.

Venice has immense beauty and sadness wrapped into one. The decline of her power and importance as a city state and as the producer of marvelous fabric has long been mourned by poets and writers, and the world has dug deep into its pockets in attempts to save her from the grasp of the sea. Tourists flock to Venice from January to December but it is not easy to live there year-round and, much as young people are attached to the city, they want a more convenient way of life without the restrictions of canals, bridges, stairways, and high water. The famous markets, which look vibrant to the outsider, are in fact declining, and Venice now faces her biggest challenge yet if she is not to become a soulless theme park.

Fagottini di crespelle

Crêpe pouches with vegetables

This recipe, with its delicate *béchamel* sauce base, works well for all kinds of vegetable, fish, and seafood fillings.

makes 8 to 10

Béchamel sauce

3 tbsp butter

3 tbsp all-purpose flour

1 ¾ cups milk, warmed

salt and black pepper

Filling

oil, for frying

12 oz zucchini, mushrooms, peppers, eggplant, pumpkin, or radicchio, diced

OR 12 oz prawns and brown crabmeat

½ oz grana padano, finely grated

salt and black pepper

Crêpes

⅓ cup 00 flour

1 large egg

1 cup milk

butter, for frying

salt and black pepper

To serve

large bunch of chives

butter

Start by making the *béchamel* sauce. Put the butter in a nonstick frying pan over medium heat. When it melts, add the flour and stir well to form a roux. Continue cooking for a minute or two, then add the warmed milk. Using a balloon whisk, stir continuously until the sauce becomes thick, smooth, and creamy. Add salt and pepper to taste.

Put enough oil to cover the base of a large frying pan over high heat, add the vegetables, and sauté until tender. Add one to two ladlefuls of the *béchamel* sauce to moisten the sautéed vegetables and reserve the rest for later use. Add the *grana padano* to the vegetable mixture and taste for seasoning. Leave to cool.

Next make the *crêpes*. Sift the flour into a large mixing bowl, make a well in the center and add the egg. Whisk, carefully working the flour into the egg, and add half of the milk, a little at a time, continuing to work the flour into the liquid. Once all the flour has been worked into the liquid, forming a thick batter, whisk well until smooth and frothy. If time allows, leave to stand for half an hour and then add the remaining milk and whisk again. Otherwise, simply add the remaining milk and whisk.

Using a small- to medium-sized frying pan, melt three to four tablespoons of butter over low heat. Pour the butter into a dish and reserve. Put the pan containing the residue of the melted butter over medium to high heat and when hot add a large spoonful of *crêpe* batter to the pan, just enough to cover the base. Swirl the mixture around to cover the base and then cook until golden brown. Flip the *crêpe* and brown on the other side. Repeat eight times to make all the *crêpes*, adding a little melted butter to the pan each time before adding the batter. It may be necessary to reduce the heat as the pan gets hotter. Stack the *crêpes* on a plate and leave to cool.

When the *crêpes* are ready, lay them out on a work surface (nicest side down) and put one tablespoon of the cooled filling in the middle of each. Using your fingers, gather the edges of each *crêpe* up around the filling and, using a chive, tie the gathers to form a pouch.

Preheat the oven to 320°F. Cover the base of a shallow oven-to-table dish with a ladleful or two of *béchamel* sauce and arrange the pouches in a single layer on top. Dot each pouch with butter and cover the dish closely with a lid or foil.

Put the dish in the oven for 20 to 30 minutes or until the sauce starts to bubble. Serve at once with extra sauce.

Piccoli carciofi con scaglie di asiago

Artichoke heart salad and asiago cheese

serves 4 or makes 18

1 tbsp mild mustard

3–4 tbsp extra virgin olive oil

juice of ½ lemon

salt and black pepper

1 tbsp finely chopped flat-leaf parsley,

4 oz asiago or grana padano shavings

4 tender young artichokes or 4 artichoke hearts in oil

baguette or filone, sliced and buttered for tartines (see page 17)

This evocative and unique dish is traditionally made with the new season's purple artichokes, from the island of Saint Erasmo in the Venetian Laguna. It is difficult to source really good fresh artichokes beyond countries such as France, Italy, and Spain. I suggest that you try using preserved artichokes—not the char-grilled variety, but the best-quality artichoke hearts in olive oil you can find.

Mix the mustard, olive oil, and lemon juice in a small bowl with a pinch of salt and a grinding of pepper to make a smooth dressing. Stir in the parsley and taste for seasoning.

Arrange the cheese shavings in piles on four plates. Peel the outer leaves from the artichokes and discard. Cut the hearts into very thin slices and toss in the dressing.

Spoon the artichoke salad on top of the cheese shavings. Alternatively, pile the cheese shavings and artichokes onto one-third-of-an-inch-thick *tartines*.

Carciofi violetta

Sautéed purple artichokes

makes 8 to 10

8 young artichokes

juice of 1 lemon

½ cup extra virgin
olive oil

1 garlic clove, finely
chopped

3 tbsp finely chopped
flat-leaf parsley

salt and black pepper

1 cup chicken stock

1 baguette or filone cut
into ½-in slices and
buttered

This evocative and unique dish is made traditionally with the
new season's purple artichokes from the island of Saint Erasmo
in the Venetian Laguna. These are nearly impossible to find outside
of Venice, so use the youngest, freshest artichokes you can get,
or preserved ones.

Pull away the tough outer leaves and trim the stem to about one inch. Using
a potato peeler, shave the tougher outer stem and the base. Cut into wedges.
Half-fill a medium bowl with cold water, and add the lemon juice. Place the
prepared artichokes in the water.

Put the olive oil in a saucepan on medium heat, add the finely chopped
garlic and two tablespoons of parsley and fry gently for a minute or so, then add
the prepared artichokes, salt and pepper. Add just enough stock to cover, put a
lid on top and cook until tender.

Reduce the stock by half or more, leaving just enough liquid to coat the
artichokes. Return the artichoke pieces to the pan and turn in the remaining
stock and add the remaining tablespoon of parsley. Put two or three artichoke
pieces on each slice of buttered bread and serve.

Tartine di crema di fave

Fava bean tartines

makes 30

1 lb shelled fava
  beans, blanched in
  salted boiling water,
  drained, and cooled

6 salted anchovy
  fillets, rinsed

a large handful of
  flat-leaf parsley,
  plus extra to serve

juice of 1 lemon

zest of ½ lemon

3–4 tbsp extra virgin
  olive oil

1 garlic clove

black pepper

1 ciabatta, cut into
  ⅓-inch slices

butter, for spreading

This combination of fava beans, anchovy, parsley, and lemon is refreshing and delicious. For a change, try omitting the anchovy fillets from the purée, and top the tartine with shavings of *asiago* or *grana padano* cheese.

Put the cooled fava beans, anchovy fillets, flat-leaf parsley, lemon zest and juice, olive oil, garlic, and black pepper in a food processor. Chop lightly, but do not reduce to a paste.

Butter the bread and put a tablespoon of the fava bean mixture on top. Add a little chopped parsley. Serve at once.

Carciofi fritti alla Giudia

Jewish-style fried artichokes

serves 6 or makes 24

3 tbsp oo flour

2 eggs

2 tbsp olive oil

salt and black pepper

6 tender artichokes
  or 3 large artichokes

4 cups sunflower oil or
  lard for frying

1 lemon cut in slices

There are many Jewish recipes in the traditional cooking of Venice, and this makes the most of one of Venice's favorite vegetables.

Put the flour in a mixing bowl, add the eggs, olive oil, salt and pepper, and beat well with a wooden spoon until smooth.

Pull away the outer leaves of the artichokes, and cut the stem to about one inch. If using older, tougher artichokes, pull off the tough outer leaves and cut off the tip of the artichoke so that it is flat. Using a potato peeler, shave the stem and the outer base. Cut into eight wedges, taking out the choke from the middle. Immerse the artichoke wedges in the batter as you cut them. Mix well.

Heat a wok or large, heavy-based pan containing the oil. When it starts to smoke, drop a crust of bread in. If the oil starts to froth around the bread and the bread turns golden, it is ready and you can start frying the artichokes in batches. Scoop out with a slotted spoon and drain on paper towels. Keep warm while frying the others, then serve piping hot with slices of lemon.

Zucca in saòr

Sweet and sour pumpkin stuzzichini

makes 30 to 40

1 pumpkin 1 lb
  in weight cut into
  8 equal pieces, seeds
  removed

2 small onions

olive oil for frying the
  onions

3 tbsp good white
  wine vinegar

4 cups sunflower oil
  for frying

¼ cup flour seasoned
  with salt and pepper

1 tbsp finely chopped
  flat-leaf parsley

30–40 wooden
  toothpicks

When the pumpkin reappears in stores, it is a sure sign that fall is around the corner. They come in many shapes and sizes but I think the big ones are best used for making seasonal lanterns. For culinary purposes use pumpkins of just of 1 lb, maximum 2 lbs, or butternut squashes, which tend to be smaller. They are easier to handle, it cooks quicker and the flesh is more succulent.

Put the prepared pumkin in a roasting tin and cook at 350°F for 30 minutes or until just tender.

While the pumpkin is cooking, slice the onions finely and sauté in a skillet over medium heat, in a little extra virgin oil until tender, do not allow them to color; this will take 10 or 15 minutes. Add the vinegar and leave to cool.

When the pumpkin is ready, leave it until cool enough to handle. Then pull the skin away from the flesh and cut the flesh into bite-size pieces.

Put the oil for frying in a deep, heavy-based pan over high heat. Put the pumpkin pieces in a large plastic bag with the seasoned flour and shake well. Discard the excess flour and then drop the floured pumpkin pieces into the bubbling oil to fry quickly; using a slotted spoon, scoop up the pieces of pumpkin as they turn golden. Transfer to paper towels to drain and then arrange on a serving platter. When all the pumpkin has been fried, cover with the prepared onion and leave to stand for at least an hour before serving. Dust with the chopped parsley.

Serve on toothpicks or in dishes.

Polpettine di melanzane

Eggplant patties

Tiny, freshly fried *polpettine* or patties are the trademark of many a Venetian *bàcaro*. As you stand quaffing your Select, Aperol, or Campari spritz, watching anonymous Veneziani idling away the time; appetizing aromas drift across the *piazza* and *polpettine* appear out of nowhere in a constant aria of ever-changing melodies: meats, fish, vegetables.

Vary the vegetables and herbs. Try pumpkin with ginger, zucchini with mint, mushrooms with flat-leaf parsley, carrot with cumin, and sweet potato with cinnamon. This is also an imaginative way of using up leftover vegetables.

Preheat the oven to 350°F. Put the eggplant on a baking tray and bake until squishy to the touch, about 20 to 30 minutes. Remove from the oven and leave to cool. Peel and squeeze out any excess moisture. Cut the eggplant into chunks and transfer to a blender or chop into small pieces. Do not reduce to mush. Transfer to a bowl and add the garlic, parsley, bread crumbs, lemon juice and zest, the egg, and the cumin or chili. Add salt and pepper to taste.

Roll teaspoons of the mixture into balls, dip in the egg and water mixture, then the flour, then the egg again, and lastly the bread crumbs. Put on a tray and put in the refrigerator until required.

Heat a wok or large heavy frying pan containing the oil. When it starts to smoke, drop a crust of bread in. If the oil starts to froth around the bread and the bread turns golden, the oil is ready and you can start frying the *polpettine* in batches.

Do not overcrowd the pan; fry six or eight at a time and transfer with a slotted spoon to paper towels to drain. Put them on a serving plate in a warm oven until all the *polpettine* are ready.

These are best served straight from the pan but you can serve them cold or reheat in a hot oven. Serve with lemon wedges.

---

makes 30

1 lb eggplant

3 garlic cloves, finely chopped

3 tbsp finely chopped flat-leaf parsley

3 oz fresh bread crumbs

juice and zest of 1 lemon

½ egg

½ tsp cumin or chili flakes

salt and black pepper

To fry

1–2 eggs, beaten with 2–4 tbsp water

½ cup flour

1 cup fresh bread crumbs

4 cups sunflower oil or lard for frying

lemon wedges, to serve

Radicchio al gorgonzola

Radicchio and gorgonzola bake

makes 18 to 24

5 oz soft gorgonzola
cheese, broken into
pieces

40 g mascarpone
galbani

2 tbsp cognac

4 heads of radicchio or
red chicory

salt and black pepper

Radicchio is another colorful vegetable synonymous with Venetian food and there are many varieties which are rarely seen beyond the region. This version was given to me by my friend Sergio who insists on the importance of keeping strictly to instructions otherwise the sauce will either split or burn.

Use this same simple *gorgonzola* base sauce to dress short pasta such as *penne*. Simply add a couple of tablespoons to heavy cream and *grana padano* to the base sauce, heat through gently, mix with the pasta and serve with extra cheese.

Preheat the oven to 400°F. Put the *gorgonzola* pieces in a small non-stick pan with the *mascarpone*. Put over low heat and, stirring constantly, melt the cheeses to a form a smooth sauce adding the brandy towards the end. The sauce should be completely smooth without lumps. Do not boil.

Transfer the sauce to a plastic container and leave to cool in the fridge; it will harden like butter.

Cut each radicchio into thin wedges and arrange in an oiled single serving ovenproof dish, add salt and pepper. Put a tablespoonful of the *gorgonzola* mixture on top. Put the four dishes on a baking tray in a hot oven for 10 minutes or until the radicchio wilts and the *gorgonzola* melts. Eat straight away.

Overleaf: Doge Francesco Foscari and the Lion of St Mark on the Doge's Palace, Venice

Risi e bisi

Risotto with peas

serves 4 or
makes 20
coffee-cup
portions

4 tbsp butter

2 tbsp extra virgin olive oil

2 shallots, finely chopped

2½ oz pancetta, finely chopped

1 handful of flat-leaf parsley, finely chopped

1½ cups vialone nanno rice or arborio rice

2 lbs fresh peas in pods

1 pinch of sugar (optional)

6 cups chicken or vegetable stock, plus 1 cup for topping up if needed

salt and black pepper

3 oz grana padano, grated, plus extra to serve

handful of mint, finely chopped (optional), to serve

This is a great favorite of mine and, like *risotto alle seppie*, it is forever associated with Venetian food. Strictly not a *cicchetto*, but rather a *primo*, it is served in small quantities, such as in a coffee cup, and it makes an elegant addition to any feast.

Risi e bisi is the pet Venetian name for *risotto con piselli*, pea *risotto*. Although, it is not traditional, I also like to add some chopped mint before serving this.

Put half the butter in a large pan with the extra virgin olive oil, and when hot add the prepared shallot, *pancetta*, and parsley and sauté gently for 10 minutes until the onion softens. Reduce the heat and add the rice and gently toast until golden.

Shell and add the peas, and when they are tender, add a pinch of sugar if using. Measure the quantity of stock, adding extra boiling water to make the mixture up to 6 cups if necessary. Add to the rice and stir well, bring back to the simmer and, stirring constantly, cook gently for 12 minutes or until the rice starts to become tender. It may be necessary to add extra stock from time to time if the rice dries out to much.

Taste, adding salt and pepper as necessary, then add the remaining butter and 2 tablespoons of grated *grana padano* and stir for a few minutes.

It is not traditional, but I like to stir in a chopping of mint before serving. Stand for a few minutes and then serve in pretty *demitasse* cups and saucers with extra *grana padano*.

La Beccheria

VENICE: MEAT

Venice is a city risen from the sea and still fighting an everlasting battle to keep it at bay. It is not surprising that fish and shellfish are at the top of the menu on the *cicchetti* board, but vegetables, cheese, and meat are not far behind.

Veal, beef, pork, and poultry are all popular meats but they do not often appear on the *cicchetto* table unless made into tiny meatballs, made either with fresh ground or leftover cooked meat. There are wonderful sausages such as *luganega* served with cabbage and *polenta*.

Today, there is a major bridge connecting Venice to the mainland, but in the past, fresh meat would have been scarce, so every bit of an animal was precious. This is one reason why offal is at the top of Venice's culinary tradition. We twenty-first-century gourmets are fairly accustomed to liver, kidney, and even tripe, but in Venice the adventurous gourmet might encounter tendons, lungs, spleen, and even more unusual delicacies.

Offal is inexpensive, and yet few people indulge these days. But give them a little oh-so-sweet Venetian chopped liver and onions, and they will rave about it until you share the astonishing secret. I urge you to try it. If you can't get calves' liver, use half chicken livers and half lamb.

Now, let us move from offal to *carpaccio*, paper-thin slices of the very finest, most tender fillet of beef served in an exquisite dressing to stimulate the appetite and satisfy the most discerning palate. Duck is also a popular meat in Venice. Poultry carcasses are dressed with the heads left on all over Italy, and one of the delightful eccentricities of the Venetian butcher's window is displaying two trussed ducks lying side by side, their heads nestling cheek to cheek.

Cotechino con funghi e polenta

Cotechino sausage with mushrooms and polenta

makes 30 plus

1 cotechino sausage

1 bay leaf

4 tbsp butter

2 garlic cloves, chopped

8 oz mixed wild mushrooms

salt and black pepper

1 handful of flat-leaf parsley, finely chopped, plus more to serve

6 oz prepared polenta (see page 16) cut into 1 x 2½ in slices

Cotechino, or *codeghino* as it is called in Venetian dialect, is a *salami*-sized sausage eaten fresh rather than matured. It is made with one-third pork rind and two-thirds lean meat and fat, each ground separately. This is then mixed together with red wine, spices, ground whole peppercorns, salt, and nitrites. The mixture is minced a second time and then made into a sausage. Boiled *cotechino* served with lentils is a festive Italian dish eaten at New Year. Lentils represent money and thus the dish is thought to bring good fortune.

You can buy *cotechino* in many authentic Italian delicatessens.

Prick the sausage skin with a fork, put in a pot, and add enough cold water to cover. Add the bay leaf and bring to a boil. Simmer for 20 minutes or according to the package instructions.

Put the butter in a large, deep frying pan, add the garlic, and put over medium heat. When the butter has melted and the garlic starts to brown, discard the garlic and add the mushrooms, salt, and pepper. Stir-fry for five to 10 minutes or until the mushrooms start to soften. Stir in the flat-leaf parsley.

Slice the cooked *cotechino* and cut each slice in half. Put a slice of *cotechino* on each slice of *polenta* and top with mushrooms and parsley.

Fasioi sofegai

Fagioli beans in peverada sauce

Peverada, or *pevarada,* is a traditional aromatic sauce that comes in many colors and is thought to date back to the medieval and Renaissance kitchens. It is made with chicken liver and *sopressa salami,* anchovies, vinegar, and fresh herbs. There are sweet and sour versions using crushed *amaretti* biscuits rather than bread crumbs, and finely chopped candied fruit, pine nuts, and golden raisins soaked in lemon juice. You can use onion rather than garlic (but not both).

The sauce is not only served with *fagioli* and other legumes but also with guinea fowl, game, chicken, pigeon, mushrooms, and kidneys. *Peverada* is an unusual combination of ingredients and flavors reflecting both the Venetian desire to waste nothing but also its glorious past and its long association with the East.

serves 4

- 9 oz fagioli beans, soaked overnight in cold water, or 2 cans of cooked fagioli tossed with a bay leaf and 3 tbsp extra virgin olive oil
- 1 slice bacon
- 1 bay leaf
- 4 oz chicken livers
- 4 oz sopressa or other top-quality salami
- 4 anchovy fillets
- handful of flat-leaf parsley or a sprig of sage, plus extra to serve
- ¼ cup extra virgin olive oil, plus extra for drizzling
- 1 garlic clove
- juice and zest of 1 lemon
- salt and black pepper
- ¼ cup good wine vinegar (red or white)
- 1 oz fresh bread crumbs
- 7 oz soft polenta (see page 16) or crusty bread

Rinse the soaked *fagioli* beans and cook in fresh water with the bacon and the bay leaf. Bring to a rapid boil, reduce the heat, and simmer until tender; about one hour. Add salt toward the end of the cooking time to taste. Alternatively, use canned *fagioli* (see ingredients list).

Finely chop the chicken livers, *salami,* anchovies, and parsley or sage.

Put a quarter of a cup of extra virgin olive oil in a pan, add a garlic clove, and cook over low–medium heat. Discard the garlic when it starts to brown, then increase the heat. Add the chopped ingredients and the grated lemon zest. Add salt and pepper and cook for five minutes. Then add the lemon juice, wine vinegar, and bread crumbs. Cook over a low heat for 20 minutes, stirring from time to time, until the sauce turns velvety.

Pour the sauce over the cooked or canned beans, stir well, then drizzle with oil and sprinkle over flat-leaf parsley and leave to stand for a few minutes before serving. Serve in individual earthenware dishes with soft *polenta* or with crusty bread.

Crostini di fegato alla veneziana

Venetian chopped liver crostini

serves 6 or
makes 40

1 tbsp olive oil

1 tbsp butter, plus
extra for spreading
or making smooth
pâté

¾ cup onion, finely
sliced

2 tbsp finely chopped
flat-leaf parsley
or marjoram, plus
extra to serve

½ lb calves' liver, or
half quantities of
the liver of your
choice and chicken
liver, thinly sliced

¼–¾ cup hot stock

salt and black pepper

1 baguette or filone cut
into slices ⅓ inch
thick

The thrifty Venetian cook wastes nothing, and offal features heavily in the traditional cooking of the city—and indeed in the whole of the Veneto region. A visit to any butcher or street market, or a glance at a traditional Venetian menu will testify to this.

As with most *crostini*, these liver *crostini* originated in order to use up leftovers of one of the most popular dishes in Venice —*il secondo* (the main course) *fegato alla veneziana*. Calves' liver is cut into domino-sized pieces and cooked with lashings of sweated onions. It looks surprisingly like our own liver and onions; however, this is where the similarity ends, as no pig's or lamb's liver can compare with the sweetness and texture of thinly sliced calves' liver.

Serve this in individual earthenware dishes or on *crostini* or *tartine* (see page 17).

Heat the oil and butter in a heavy saucepan over low heat; stir in the onion and parsley or marjoram, and cover. Cook gently for 50 minutes, adding a little water from time to time to prevent brown or burning.

Cut the liver into pieces roughly the size of dominoes. When the onion is very soft, increase the heat and add the liver, turning it quickly to seal in the flavor. Add the stock and simmer for two to three minutes. Add plenty of seasoning, stir, and taste.

Strain off any excess liquor. Transfer the liver and onion to a board and chop into grain-size pieces with a knife. Serve on *tartine* of crusty buttered bread or *crostoni* topped with a little parsley or marjoram.

If you prefer a velvety smooth *pâté*, reduce the ingredients to a paste in a blender and add half their weight in softened butter. Transfer the *pâté* to parchment paper, roll into a *salami*-shaped cylinder, and refrigerate until set. Serve sliced on *tartine* and garnish with freshly chopped herbs.

Overleaf: Chioggia Delta Po parkland leading to a Venetian lagoon

Polpettine di manzo

Meatballs made with beef

makes 30

8 oz finely ground
beef, cooked or raw

8 oz potatoes, boiled,
peeled, and put
through a potato
ricer

2 oz sopressa or
speck, minced

2 garlic cloves, minced

2–3 heaped tbsp finely
chopped marjoram
or flat-leaf parsley

1 tbsp tomato paste

salt and black pepper

½ egg, to bind

To fry

1 egg, plus 2–4 tbsp
cold water

½ cup all-purpose
flour

¾–1 cup dried bread
crumbs

5 cups sunflower oil
or lard, for frying

Polpettine come in myriad forms in the firmament of *bàcari cicchetti*. They appear freshly made from a hatch in the wall in a constant stream straight from the kitchen, as if produced on a *polpette* conveyor belt. Some are made with fresh meat, raw vegetables, or raw fish, and others are made with leftover meat, cooked fish, or vegetables. This recipe works with both fresh and leftover beef.

This recipe calls for boiled potato to be added to the meat, but other recipes use bread soaked in milk or dried bread crumbs. The important thing is to grind the beef twice to ensure the filling is soft and smooth. The addition of finely chopped *sopressa* or *speck* adds depth of flavor and texture to the mixture.

Put the beef, cooled potato purée, *sopressa*, garlic, marjoram or parsley, tomato paste, salt, pepper, and half an egg in a bowl. Mix well with your hands.

Crack open the egg into a large bowl, add the water, and whisk gently with a fork. Put the flour in a large bowl and the bread crumbs in another bowl.

Roll a teaspoon of the mixture into a ball, dust in the flour, dip in the egg mixture, and then roll in the bread crumbs. Arrange them on a tray and put in the refrigerator until required.

Heat a wok or large, heavy pan containing the oil. When it starts to smoke, drop a crust of bread into it. If the oil starts to froth around the bread and turn golden, it is ready. Fry the *polpettine* in batches of six to eight to avoid overcrowding the pan. Use a slotted spoon to transfer them onto paper towels to drain. Move the *polpettine* to a serving plate in a warm oven until the others are ready.

These are best served straight from the pan, but you can serve them cold or reheat in a hot oven.

Polenta con luganega e cavolo capuccio

Luganega sausage and cabbage polenta pots

serves 2 or
makes 12

1–2 tsp butter

½ lb luganega or
other sausage, cut
in half lengthwise

2 large sage leaves,
finely chopped

4 oz finely shredded
cabbage

2 tbsp white wine
vinegar

polenta, already
prepared (see
page 16)

1 tsp finely chopped
sage leaves

Luganega is a fine-cut sausage from the Veneto, encased in a delicate skin and made with the best cuts of lean meat and *lardo*. It is flavored with salt, black pepper, and garlic, and eaten freshly made rather than matured.

This is not strictly a *cicchetto*, but a variation on a very Venetian theme. Corn is one of the two staple crops (the other is rice) grown across the Veneto region, and consequently, both *polenta* and rice dishes abound. *Polenta* is traditionally made in a copper pan. The *polenta* flour is jettisoned into a pan of bubbling water, stirred until almost solid, and then turned out on a board and cut with a wire.

There is a modern trend toward making a lighter, softer, creamier *polenta*, often with fresh herbs, which I find altogether more enjoyable.

Melt the butter in a frying pan over low heat, then increase the heat and add the sausages and sage. Fry until brown and then add the cabbage leaves, mixing well until the cabbage starts to wilt. Add the vinegar, and mix again. Serve with soft *polenta* flavored with finely chopped fresh sage leaves in small terra-cotta dishes if available.

Carpaccio di manzo al asiago

Carpaccio of beef fillet with asiago cheese

serves 4

8 oz trimmed fillet
steak or fillet steak
tail

salt and black pepper

juice of ½ lemon

3 oz arugula

2 oz asiago or grana
padano cheese
shavings

extra virgin olive oil,
(from Lake Garda if
possible)

In the mid-twentieth century, Giuseppe Cipriani, founder of Harry's Bar in Venice, created a new dish of paper-thin fillet steak dressed with a mayonnaise sauce. At that time there was an exhibition in the city featuring the work of Venetian painter Carpaccio. Seeing a blood-red poster advertising the show, Cipriani seized on the name for his dish. Since then, raw meat dishes known as *crudi* have also been referred to as *carpaccios*.

Carpaccio is not a *cicchetto*, but it is as Venetian as any *cicchetto*, and thus is the perfect dish for sharing. Try serving *carpaccio cicchetti*-style on *tartine* with arugula and *asiago* cheese. Make and serve them straight away!

Using a meat slicer or a very sharp knife, cut the meat into paper-thin slices. Arrange them on four plates in a single layer and add salt, pepper, and lemon juice.

Pile the arugula on top and add the *asiago* cheese shavings. Drizzle with extra virgin olive oil and eat at once.

Left: Polenta con luganega e cavolo capuccio

Tripa in umido con polenta

Tripe, tomato, and porcini mushroom stew with polenta

serves 6 or
makes 36

²/₃ cup fagioli beans,
soaked overnight in
cold water

1 bay leaf

1 piece of grana
padano rind

1 lb tripe

1 tbsp butter

2 oz lardo, bacon
fat, or pancetta,
finely chopped

1 small carrot, finely
chopped

1 celery stalk, finely
chopped

1 small onion, finely
chopped

3 tomatoes, skinned,
deseeded, and
chopped

4 oz dried porcini
mushrooms, soaked
for 10 minutes in
warm water and
drained

2 ladlefuls of pork of
vegetable stock

2 potatoes, peeled
and cut into small
cubes

salt and black pepper

To serve

polenta, sliced (see
page 16)

grana padana,
grated

flat-leaf parsley,
finely chopped

Offal plays an important role in Venetian popular cooking and features on many traditional *osteria* and *cicchetteria* menus. *Nervetti* (chopped up tendons and meat from the foot of a calf), *rumegal* (a part of the cow's stomach), and *spiensa* or *milza* (spleen) are three popular examples.

Always game to sample the traditional fare, I have eaten my way through a plate of very chewy *nervetti* and nibbled on a boiled *milza cicchetto*, which was so unpalatable I discouraged my companion from trying it. I have yet to be offered *rumegal* because it is no longer very popular.

The tradition of eating offal in Venice is, like elsewhere, fading. However, dishes such as liver and onions and tripe will, I imagine, never lose their popularity. So I include a tripe recipe here. Make this dish as a main course and use up any leftovers for *cicchetti*.

Rinse the soaked *fagioli* beans, cover with fresh cold water in a large pot, and add a bay leaf and a piece of *grana padano* rind. Bring to a boil and simmer for 30 minutes until tender. Drain and set aside. Rinse the tripe, put it in another pot, cover with cold water, bring to a boil, and simmer for 40 minutes until tender. Drain and cut the tripe into slivers.

Put the butter and the *lardo* or bacon fat in a large pan with the carrot, celery, and onion, and cook over medium heat until the vegetables are soft. Add the tomatoes, mushrooms, tripe, and stock, and cook over low heat for 40 minutes to create a rich sauce. Add the potatoes and the drained beans and cook for a further 40 minutes.

Serve in individual earthenware dishes on slices of *polenta* sprinkled with *grana padano* and chopped parsley.

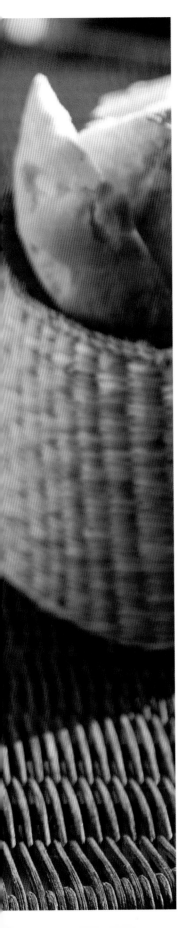

Il Bàcaro

VENICE: APERITIVI

It is said that the people of the Veneto region will always find a good reason to drink a glass of wine or an *aperitivo*. What a wonderful ethos! They even have their own word for such a relaxing drink: *ombra*, which means "shade" and relates to when portable wine bars used to follow the shadow of the Campanile bell tower across St. Mark's Square. The range of wines and drinks from the area is awesome, and many of the unique, regional wines are household names the world over: *valpolicella, prosecco, soave, amarone, bardolino, bianco di custoza, rossi di garda*. All of them conjure up the flavors and landscape of the region. Drink them by the glass at the *bàcaro* with some *cicchetti* or enjoy them by the bottle with a meal.

Not least of all are the cocktails of Veneto, including the Bellini and the Rossini; the *aperitivi* such as Cynar, Aperol, Select, and Campari; and sodas and the spritz. All their recipes are indelibly scribed in the ether of every *bàcaro* in the region.

Bellini

makes 6

3 ripe white peaches,
    peeled and stoned

3 cups well-chilled
    prosecco

Memories are made of this wonderful, sensual summer drink. It was invented in Harry's Bar in Venice, and made with two simple ingredients—white peaches and *prosecco*. The peaches must be fresh, ripe, and juicy and the *prosecco* must be the very finest. I tasted my first Bellini at Villa Cipriani, a glorious hotel in romantic Asolo.

Not so many years ago *prosecco* was unheard of beyond the confines of the Veneto region and the Venetian *bàcari*. The quality was consistent then; a light, smooth, barely fruity fizz with the softest of foamy bubbles. But since it has become the fizz of choice everywhere, the quality has become variable depending on the producer. If you are lucky enough to find a *prosecco* brand that has a string-tied cork you are probably onto a good thing.

Put the peaches in a blender, reduce to a purée, and chill. Divide the peach purée between six champagne or cocktail glasses, top with *prosecco*, swizzle, and serve.

Variation:

Make a Bellini Rossini using a handful of strawberries instead of white peaches.

Campari sour

serves 1

1 part lemon juice

1 part superfine sugar

1½ parts Campari

lemon-lime soda

1 strawberry

1 lime wedge

Campari with ice and soda, topped with a wedge of lime, is my regular summer drink. On special occasions I omit the soda and add a measure of gin. When the cocktail shaker makes an appearance, I love a Campari cocktail (and there are many). Try this simple Campari sour. You can make it with other Italian bitters, such as amber-colored Aperol, adding a mixture of orange and lemon juice.

Fill a cocktail glass with ice and leave to stand while you make the sour. Put a tumbler full of ice in a cocktail shaker, add the lemon juice, sugar, and Campari, and shake well. Pour the ice out of the cocktail glass and add the strained contents of the cocktail shaker to the glass. Top the glass off with a thread of lemon-lime soda. Add a strawberry and a lime wedge to the rim of the glass, and serve.

Negroni

serves 1

1 part sweet vermouth

1 part Campari

1 part gin

1 orange wedge (skin on, pips removed)

Negroni is an elegant Campari cocktail made for savoring on a long summer evening or before a relaxing lunch.

Fill a glass with ice, swizzle, and stand for two minutes. Pour off any excess water before adding the vermouth, Campari, and gin. Swizzle and top with the orange wedge.

Variation:

For a change, try mixing one part dry vermouth, one part Aperol, and one part amaretto with a lime wedge.

Right: Negroni

Overleaf: Vineyards in the prosecco region

Lo spritz da Florian

The Florian spritz

serves 1

1 measure of chilled
bitter Select

1 glass of chilled
prosecco

still or sparkling water,
(optional)

Myriad visitors to Venice will have marveled at the beautiful Caffe Florian in Piazza San Marco, either for the cost of its drinks or for its elegance. If you take a look behind the bar, the bottle of bitter Select takes pride of place on the shelf over both Aperol and Campari, and this is why I have called this drink the Florian spritz. Caffe Florian's actual formula is of course a well-kept secret.

As I tell everyone who is not used to Italian bar etiquette, the rules are quite simple. If you want to sit down and revel in the surroundings of a world-famous café in an iconic piazza you will pay dearly for the pleasure. However, once you have sat down and ordered your "spritz con Select" you can sit and people-watch and wallow in the romance of the surroundings for as long as you like. Think of the bill as a ticket to a world-famous theater.

Pour a measure of Select into a large, beautiful glass, add the *prosecco*, and sparkling water if desired.

Lo spritz Triestino

The Trieste spritz

serves 1

²⁄₃ cup white or
red wine

¹⁄₃ cup sparkling water

This is the original spritz created by Austrian soldiers not used to drinking the strong wines of the Veneto. How much water you add to the wine is up to you. The basic formula is a measure of wine poured into a tumbler and topped off with sparkling water. The finer points are up to you, but I have made a basic suggestion by including measures in the ingredients list.

Left: Lo spritz da Florian

Lo spritz Padovano

The Padova spritz

serves 1

1 measure chilled
bitter Cynar

chilled white wine

sparkling water

2–3 ice cubes

One of the great pleasures of Venice is taking a stroll in the early evening through the piazzas and meeting with friends for a drink before dinner.

Pour a measure of Cynar into a glass, and add the white wine, sparkling water, and ice as desired.

Spritzissimo

The ultimate spritz

serves 1

½ measure of 2
of the following:
Cynar, Aperol,
Campari, Select,
Bianco Sarti

½ measure of chilled
Plymouth Gin

½ glass of proseco or
Manzoni

chilled sparkling water
(optional)

2–3 ice cubes

This is spritz gone mad: two types (or more) of bitters fortified with gin and lightened with white wine, *prosecco*, or a cross-breed such as Manzoni.

You are sure to enjoy the unique taste of this cool spritz on a hot summer day, whether you are lucky enough to be sitting at a table in a Venetiam piazza or not. The amount of sparkling water, choice of bitters and number of ice cubes are all up to you so experiment and enjoy at your leisure.

Put the half measures of two of the bitters in a large glass, add the gin, then the wine or *prosecco*. Top off with sparkling water if desired and add ice cubes.

Left: Lo spritz Padovano

Lo spritz Veneziano

The Venetian spritz

serves 1

½ measure of chilled Aperol or Campari

½ glass of chilled white wine

chilled sparkling water (optional)

2–3 ice cubes

twist of orange zest for Aperol or lime zest for Campari

This is a light spritz made simply with white wine and either amber Aperol or crimson Campari. It is the drink I most associate with the *bàcari* in the Rialto district. The actual quantities are up to you, but I have listed my own preferences here.

Pour the bitters into a large wine chalice, add the wine, and top off with a quarter to a third of a cup of sparkling water if desired, and top with the citrus zest of choice.

Sgroppino con prosecco

Lemon sorbet with prosecco and vodka

serves 1

1 scoop lemon sorbet

1 tbsp chilled grappa or vodka

chilled prosecco

Today *sgroppino* comes in many variations but originally it was simply a lemon sorbet with *grappa* poured over it, served as a digestive after a meal. The word *sgroppino* comes from *sgroppare, sciogliere il nodo*, to undo the knot or to facilitate the digestion. I somehow have my doubts that a dose of ice-cold sorbet aids the digestion more than a simple measure of *grappa* on its own, but it is a delicious way to finish a meal if you, like me, love *grappa*.

Put a large scoop of sorbet in a glass, add the *grappa* or vodka, and top the glass off with *prosecco*. Serve with a straw and a teaspoon.

Right: Sgroppino con prosecco

Lo spritz Trevigiano

The Treviso spritz

serves 1

1 green olive or
  1 cocktail cherry

1 measure of chilled
  Aperol or Campari

chilled prosecco

I like to keep my *prosecco* spritz fully leaded and not watered down. Again, quantities vary according to taste; this is my suggestion.

Put an olive for Aperol or a cocktail cherry for Campari in the bottom of a cocktail glass, add the bitters, and top off with *prosecco*.

Vov

makes 4 cups

1¼ cups milk

11 oz sugar

1 vanilla pod,
  split open with a
  sharp knife

6 egg yolks

1¼ cups Marsala

¾ cup of 90-proof
  alcohol or ½ cup
  vodka if using OR
  2 measures of
  brandy (optional)

Vov is a popular homemade drink all over Italy but it comes originally from the Veneto region. Its name originates from the regional dialectal word *vovi*, meaning eggs. What a drink! *Marsala*, eggs, vanilla, and sugar make it almost a *zabaione* in a bottle. Drink hot or cold; enjoy straight away or bottled.

The original recipe contains 90-proof alcohol, which is readily available in Italy for making homemade liqueurs. Sadly, it is not easy to come by elsewhere. It is probably best made by adding a little brandy to give it a kick and drinking it straight away. Alternatively, you could add a spirit such as vodka to help preserve it.

Gently heat the milk in a saucepan with eight and ¾ of an ounce of the sugar and the vanilla pod. When it begins to simmer, take the pan off the heat. Leave the vanilla to infuse until the mixture is quite cold.

Put the egg yolks in a large bowl with the remaining sugar and whisk until the whisk leaves a trail. Add the *marsala* and the alcohol (if using) and beat again. Whisk in the cold milk. Strain and bottle in stone jars, which will keep for eight days before using.

If you want to drink this straight away, instead of adding the alcohol, add a couple of measures of brandy and serve in pretty glasses.

Left: Vov

Lo spritz-analcolico

The mock-spritz

serves 1

1 lump of preserved
   ginger in syrup

¼ an orange

chilled Crodino

1 lime wedge

Fill a cocktail glass with ice and leave to stand for two minutes. Pour away the ice, and add a small lump of preserved ginger in syrup and the juice of the orange.

Top off with Crodino and hang a lime wedge on the rim of the glass.

Grappa con i semi di cumino

Cumin seed-flavored grappa

makes 4 cups

4¼ cups grappa

7 oz cumin seeds

There is a great tradition of making flavored liqueurs at home in Italy, and they are very easy to make. All manner of spices, herbs, and flowers are macerated for weeks on end. The product is then filtered through muslin to clear it, and bottled. Cumin is a popular flavoring, as it is known to aid digestion. You can experiment with other flavorings and spirits. For mint-flavored *grappa*, add 10 large mint sprigs; for chamomile-flavored *grappa*, add a handful of freshly dried flowers. This drink is one for the connoisseur, though.

Put the seeds in a bottle, add the *grappa*, and leave for 60 days. Filter, transfer to a clean bottle, and seal.

Right: Grappa con i semi di cumino

ABRUZZO & MOLISE

The pairing of these two southern regions started in Roman times; together they formed the Fourth Roman Region. After the fall of Rome, Molise went on to suffer a tremendously tortured period of history, being passed from hand to hand by the Longobards, Saracens, and Byzantines, and ending up a Norman possession under Frederick II. This was followed by years of misery and deprivation before Molise finally rejoined Abruzzo in 1860. In 1963 the two regions were divided once again for good, although in most people's minds they remain forever joined.

They share a similar landscape, though the Abruzzi is more mountainous and densely wooded than Molise, which makes agriculture difficult.

In addition to locality, the traditions and gastronomic specialties born of sheep farming link the two areas. The food is quite similar in both regions, although the famous *chitarra*, which is used to make thick, square spaghetti cut by the steel strings stretched taut over a hollow box, is absolutely Abruzzese.

The entire region of the Abruzzi is mountainous and cut by deep green basins. The highest Apennine peaks of the Gran Sasso Massif soar up from lean pastures and scraggy woods. It's a grandiose and awe-inspiring view, which is both desolate and uplifting at the same time. The valleys are green, gentle, and rich, sweetened by the rivers and streams, and then there is yet another sharp contrast: the jump from mountains to seashore. As the crow flies, only 30 miles separate the Abruzzi's highest mountain peaks from the sandy shores of its coastline.

Whether it is pork, lamb, mutton, or seafood, the common denominator in most of the local specialties is the use of a fiery dried chili pepper, known as *pepedinie*. It seems to find its way into everything from the fish soup of Pescara, (which requires 15 whole chilis for just six portions), to the delicious pork *salami* and tomato sauces for pasta.

The most interesting Abruzzese culinary tradition is *La Panarda*, a multicourse feast of gargantuan proportions. A legend holds that *La Panarda* was born when a young mother, gone to fetch water near her home, returned to find her newborn in the mouth of a wolf. Desperate, the woman prayed to Saint Anthony of Abate, and the wolf let the baby go. The grateful young mother promised to prepare a feast for Saint Anthony, starting a tradition that would be passed down from generation to generation for centuries to come. Most *Panarde* consist of 35 to 50 courses and last all night, thus enabling guests to partake of every dish at a leisurely pace.

In contrast to the Abruzzi's relative success throughout history, Molise feels much more remote and gives the impression that it is still waiting to be properly discovered. The main city is Campobasso, famous since the fourteenth century for the creation of blades (especially scissors). It lies in the high basin of the Biferno River, which has long been famous for the production of pears and *scamorza* cheese.

Among the region's best products, extra virgin olive oil, the Isernia truffle, and durum wheat pasta stand out. One of Italy's most loved and respected brands of durum wheat pasta is called *La Molisana*.

There are several types of *salami*, including *saggicciotti* liver sausage, *ventricina salami*, and *pampanera* oven-dried bacon infused with chili pepper.

Ewe's milk and cow's milk products are extremely popular in this region, in particular the *caciocavallo* and *stracciata* cheeses of Agnone and Alto Molise; *fior di latte*, cow's milk *mozzarella*, from Boiano; buffalo *mozzarella* from Venafro; and *pecorino* in various stages of maturity. *Scamorza* cheese and *burrino*, a butter-filled cheese, are produced everywhere in Molise.

Rotolini alla crema di fave

Stuffed mini pancakes with fava bean cream

For a rich marriage of flavors and textures, try these creamy egg pancakes, *frittatine*.

serves 4

8 oz fava beans, fresh or frozen

2 tbsp robiola or similar cream cheese

1 tbsp grated pecorino

4 eggs

3 tbsp milk

1 tbsp all-purpose flour

2–3 tbsp finely chopped flat-leaf parsley

salt and black pepper

2 tbsp sunflower oil

4 slices prosciutto cotto (Italian cooked ham) or boiled ham, halved

2–3 basil sprigs

Boil the fava beans until softened in lightly salted water for six minutes. Drain, cool, and place in the food processor with the cream cheese and *pecorino* and blend until smooth. Season to taste.

Beat the eggs in a bowl with the milk, flour, flat-leaf parsley, and some salt and pepper.

In a lightly oiled, nonstick pan, use this mixture to make about eight small, flat, thin omelettes (*frittatine*), cooking them on each side for about four minutes. Make sure they are cooked through but soft enough to roll up. Leave to cool.

Lay a slice of ham on top of each little pancake and spread with the fava bean and cheese mixture, then roll up and cut across into bite-sized pieces, sealing each one safely closed with a wooden toothpick.

Chill until required and garnish with the basil sprigs just before serving.

Cipolline al cacao

Cocoa-dusted baby onions

This recipe has a very unusual combination of flavors, but one that works really well, especially with red wine or even mulled wine. This is a much less rich version of a very similar recipe that crops up farther north in Liguria and Piedmont, often as part of a large array of different *antipasto* dishes.

serves 4

4 tbsp unsalted butter

28 oz ready-peeled baby onions (pickling or borettana variety)

1 pinch of salt

3 tbsp white wine vinegar

¼ cup dry white wine

1 tbsp unsweetened cocoa powder

1 tbsp superfine sugar

Melt the butter in a pan over medium heat and add the onions. Allow to brown slightly all over, then season with salt.

Add the vinegar and wine and cook gently for about 10 minutes, stirring.

Raise the heat to allow all the liquid to evaporate once the onions are softened but not falling apart. Leave to cool slightly.

Just before serving, dust the warm onions with the cocoa powder and the sugar, push a wooden toothpick into each one, and serve.

Right: Rotolini alla crema di fave

Tartine di crema di asparagi

Creamed asparagus tartine

makes 30

1 lb asparagus

4 free-range eggs, hard-boiled and finely chopped or mashed

3 tbsp extra virgin olive oil

2 tbsp mayonnaise

salt and black pepper

1 fresh filone or baguette cut into ¼-in slices and buttered

This recipe calls for green asparagus. When choosing asparagus, make sure the spears are more or less all the same diameter and length and that they are bright green, firm, and are freshly picked.

Bring a large, deep frying pan of water to a boil, and add salt to taste. Cut off the tough part at the base of the spears and discard. Carefully immerse the asparagus in boiling water and simmer until just tender, four to five minutes, and test for tenderness with a fork. Drain, immerse in cold water, and leave to cool. Cut off the tips and reserve. Chop the spears finely.

Put the chopped egg in a bowl with the chopped asparagus, olive oil, and mayonnaise. Season with salt and pepper to taste and mix carefully.

Spread the mixture on the buttered bread, top each one with an asparagus tip, and serve at once.

Cazzimperio

Rich melted cheese on toast

serves 6

1 lb 3 oz caciocavallo

2 cups whole milk

9 tbsp unsalted butter

5 egg yolks

¾ cup all-purpose flour

salt and black pepper

6 large slices of two-day-old crusty Italian bread (casareccio)

This is the Abruzzese version of cheese on toast, and it can be made with any tasty leftover bits of cheese you might have that are suitable for melting. On the other hand, if you wanted to be really traditional, you need to use *caciocavallo*, which is a kind of *provolone* made all over Southern Italy but especially in the Appennines.

Cut the cheese into small cubes, place in a bowl, and cover completely with the milk. Leave to soak overnight.

Next day, beat the butter into a creamy consistency with the egg yolks and the flour. Stir the soaked cheese and the milk into this mixture.

Pour into a heavy-bottomed, wide pan and melt very gently over a low heat until smooth, stirring frequently.

Toast the bread on both sides in a chargrill pan until crisp and lightly browned. Slice into halves or quarters, and then arrange on a dish. Coat each slice generously with the melted cheese mixture and serve immediately.

Right: Tartine di crema di asparagi

Tortine al formaggio

Mint, garlic, and ricotta pockets

serves 8 or
makes about
24

5⅓ cups all-purpose
flour

1 cup cold water

1 lb ricotta

1 large sprig of mint,
very finely chopped

2 garlic cloves,
crushed

1 egg

salt and black pepper

4 cups sunflower oil

This simple dish of garlicky, mint-scented *ricotta* pockets comes from the regional capital of Molise, the city called Campobasso.

Tip the flour out onto the work surface and add the water gradually to make a smooth, elastic dough.

Allow the dough to rest for 10 minutes, then roll it out thinly and evenly on a lightly floured surface with a well floured rolling pin to a thickness of about a quarter of an inch. Cut into circles (about two inches across) using a cookie cutter or an upturned glass. You should get at least 24 circles out of the mixture.

In a bowl, mix together the *ricotta* with the mint, garlic, and egg. Season with salt and pepper.

Place a little spoonful of this mixture in the center of each circle of dough, fold over to seal, and press closed with your fingertips or the tines of a fork.

Heat a wok or large, heavy-based pan containing the oil. When it starts to smoke, drop a crust of bread in. If the oil starts to froth around the bread and the bread turns golden, it is ready and you can start frying the pasties in batches.

Remove the crisp, cooked pasties from the hot oil, drain on paper towels, and serve piping hot.

Nocciole fritte

Pan-fried hazelnuts

serves 4

1 cup hazelnuts

2 eggs, beaten

4 tbsp semola or
very fine semolina

2 cups sunflower oil

This is one of the simplest little snacks I have ever come across. Once I was served it in the home of friends in the lovely city of L'Aquila, and I was completely hooked! Make sure the hazelnuts are fresh and that the thin brown skin inside the shell has been carefully removed before you begin. *Semola* is hard wheat (durum wheat) flour, but very fine *semolina* or even fine *polenta* flour will also work in this recipe.

Roll the hazelnuts in the egg then *semola* or *semolina* to coat. Shake off any excess *semola* using a sieve.

Heat the oil in a wide frying pan until sizzling. Add the coated nuts, in batches, and allow them to fry for just two minutes before removing with a slotted spoon and draining on paper towels.

Serve piping hot.

Left: Tortine al formaggio dough

BASILICATA

This region was first called Lucania, and took its name from the early inhabitants, the Lucani. Under the Byzantines it was renamed Basilicata (from the Greek word *basilikos*, which gave an indication of the governor's standing). The name stuck throughout a long period of Norman rule, and then between 1932 and 1947 it was renamed Lucania. Nowadays, it is once again called Basilicata, although its citizens are still Lucani!

The region's cuisine makes good use of the land and the meat from sheep rearing (and also the sheep dairy products) and pig keeping. Fish is difficult to find throughout the region, apart from along the coast.

The flavors of the local food are robust, sharp, and intense. Pork, durum wheat pasta and bread, and vegetables are the stars of the table. But beneath the tranquil surface of Basilicata's quiet exterior, a cuisine rages with the heat of the *peperoncino*, the fiery chili pepper.

Salsicce Lucane, or *Lucanica*, is the pork sausage of Basilicata, and it is made using only top-quality meat seasoned with fennel seeds, salt, and pepper or *peperoncino*. The name *Lucanica* (a type of continuous, coiled sausage), which is widely used in northern Italy, was in all probability born here. The local *Lucanica* is flavored with black pepper and chili. It has a strong, almost aggressive, taste, and is eaten fresh, roasted, fried, preserved in oil, or smoked and left to dry.

The *peperone di Senise* is cultivated in a number of villages in the heart of Basilicata. This includes Senise, the village that gives the pepper its name, which stands on the slopes of a hill in the valley of the River Sinni. Traditionally used for flavoring peasant dishes, the Senise pepper is a specialty of the Basilicata region and has been produced with IGP status (Protected Geographical Indication) since 1996. Brick red in color, the Senise pepper can be eaten fresh. It has a slightly elongated form and very thin flesh, and because it contains very little water, it is particularly well suited to being dried and turned into powder. In powdered form, the Senise pepper is often used for making local cheeses and cured meats, and for flavoring soups and stews. In dialect, it is known as *crusch*.

A very typical dish of the Basilicata region is lamb, mutton, or kid cooked in a *pignata*, or a deep earthenware pot. The dish is flavored with bread crumbs, carrots, cheese, and sausage, or is *al cuturillo*, meaning "cooked with chicory."

Pork is a fundamental element in the local cuisine. This is because a pig can be reared anywhere, and because every bit of one can be used; even the blood is used for making the well-known local dessert *sanguinaccio*. The Lucano pig is generally thin, since it pastures on the mountains together with sheep and lambs. These scrawny pigs yield a ham that is dry and sinewy, wonderfully spicy, and full of flavor. There are also sausages made from a finely minced mixture, *soppressata salamis*, *capocollo* hams, and the typical *pezzente* ("beggar") sausage, so called because it was eaten by the poorest people. Composed of the scraps from the slaughterhouse (lungs, liver, veins), chopped into tiny pieces, and flavored with generous quantities of pepper and garlic, it is utterly delicious.

Another key element of this simple gastronomy is bread. Durum wheat *semolina* is the overall base of practically all the relevant preparations both for bread and pasta. The great majority of pasta or bread dishes in the region use this ancient cereal as their main ingredient, and it is has been cultivated here from time immemorial.

The most famous bread is *matera*, one of the most unusual and most delicious types of bread produced in the south of Italy. It is made in huge loaves that remain soft and tasty for several days. Local housewives would prepare their own loaves and take them to the communal oven for baking. In order to recognize one's own loaf, it was stamped with a distinguishing mark, a symbol, or the initials of the family. Traditionally, *matera* has always been baked in a stone oven, fired by oak, and the loaves weigh up to 11 pounds or more. Historically, when the locals were taxed for the use of the ovens, the tax was levied according

Right: Night cityscape of Matera, Basilicata

to the number of loaves, irrespective of size or weight. So the wily citizens of *matera* made sure they baked loaves of enormous size and created dough that produced bread that stayed fresh for longer.

Out of the spotlight for centuries, the local farming community has developed cooking skills made up of ancient teachings, time-tested recipes, and culinary customs tied to the oldest and most traditional beliefs.

Frittelle Lucane

Lucanian fritters

serves 4

2¼ cups water

1 bay leaf

3 tbsp olive oil

1¾ cups all-purpose flour

1 tbsp semolina

4 cups sunflower oil

confectioners' sugar, for dusting (optional)

sea salt

Another one of those examples of *cucina povera*, this is a very simple yet delicious dish that can be served as sweet or savory.

Bring the water to a boil in a saucepan, with the bay leaf, olive oil, and a little salt, then add the flour and *semolina*, stirring constantly to make sure the mixture remains smooth and lump-free. Traditionally, you should stir in a figure-eight motion to make sure the spoon always crosses the center of the pan.

After about 10 minutes, when the mixture is cooked, tip it out onto a slightly dampened, shallow tray and smooth it out with a palette knife to make sure it is all the same thickness (about one inch). Discard the bay leaf. Leave to cool and set.

Once cool, slice into rectangles.

Heat a wok or large, heavy-based pan containing the oil. When it starts to smoke, drop a crust of bread in. If the oil starts to froth around the bread and the bread turns golden, it is ready and you can start frying the rectangles in batches for three to four minutes. Drain on paper towels to remove any excess oil. Sprinkle with confectioners' sugar or salt and serve hot.

Bocconcini di verdure

Vegetable fritters

serves 4

2 eggs

1 pinch of salt

½ tsp black pepper

1 cup all-purpose flour

⅓ cup milk

1½ tsp baking powder

2 zucchini, sliced into thick rounds

½ cauliflower, split into florets

4 baby artichokes, trimmed

4¼ cups sunflower oil

sea salt

This very old recipe from the Basilicata region is rather like an Italian version of vegetables fried in tempura batter.

Beat the eggs, salt, and pepper together and gradually sift in the flour, alternating with the milk, until you have a smooth, thick batter. Whisk in the baking powder last of all.

Wash the vegetables carefully. Bring a large pan of salted water to a boil and cook all the vegetables until just tender. Drain thoroughly and set aside to cool.

Heat the oil in a lage pan until sizzling, then dip the vegetables into the batter to coat thoroughly, and drop into the hot oil to fry until puffed up and golden brown; about three to four minutes.

Remove the cooked fritters and drain carefully on paper towels to remove excess oil. Sprinkle lightly with sea salt and serve piping hot.

Right: Bocconcini di verdure

Polpettini di pane

Fried bread patties

These delicious little fried bread balls are another example of real *cucina povera*, the ability to make something special out of very little. The secret for success is to use really tasty, good-quality bread, even if it is hard and stale.

serves 4

1 lb 1 oz stale bread

1 cup milk

3 eggs

5 oz pecorino, grated

1 small onion, finely chopped

2 tbsp finely chopped flat-leaf parsley

2 tbsp parmesan, grated

salt and black pepper

6 tbsp dried, fine bread crumbs

4¼ cups sunflower oil

Moisten the bread in the milk until soft, breaking it up with your hands as it becomes soft. You may need to use a little more milk if the bread is really dry and hard.

Beat two of the eggs and mix the crumbled moist (but not soaking) bread with the beaten eggs, then mix in the *pecorino*, onion, flat-leaf parsley, *parmesan*, salt, and pepper. Shape into golf ball-sized patties.

Beat the third egg into a shallow dish and measure the bread crumbs into another bowl. Roll the patties in the egg then into the bread crumbs to coat completely. Shake off any excess bread crumbs.

Heat a wok or large, heavy-based pan containing the oil. When it starts to smoke, drop a crust of bread in. If the oil starts to froth around the bread and the bread turns golden, it is ready and you can start frying the patties in batches for three to four minutes on each side. Drain on paper towels to remove any excess oil and serve ar once.

Cruschi fritti

Fried sun-dried peppers

The dark and wrinkly sun-dried peppers come from the area around the town of Senise. They have a thin flesh that makes them perfect for drying. Locals will say you can tell at once if they are the real thing if they remain crisp after careful frying. These peppers are really deliciously sweet and very special, a true symbol of the food of Basilicata.

serves 4

8 cruschi peppers

2½ cups olive oil

sea salt

Split the peppers in half lengthwise, and wipe with a dry cloth.

Heat a wide frying pan containing the oil. When it starts to smoke, drop a crust of bread in. If the oil starts to froth around the bread and the bread turns golden, it is ready and you can fry the peppers, for no longer than one minute.

Drain on paper towels to remove excess oil, sprinkle lightly with a little salt to taste, and serve at once.

Left: Polpettini di pane

Capocolle di Basilicata e caciocavallo

Basilicata salami and caciocavallo cheese

serves 4

extra virgin olive oil

6 oz caciocacallo
cheese, cold from
the fridge cut into
10 or 12 equal sized
batons

10–12 slices thinly
sliced capocolle

polenta crostini (see
page 16)

few sprigs of
rosemary

A wonderful combination of two great regional specialties. *Capocolle* is a *salume* made from pork neck and shoulder, and *caciocavalle* is a delicious and unusual cheese. If you can't find *caciocavalle*, you can substitute a smoked *mozzarella*.

Grease a baking tray, and preheat the oven to 400°F. Wrap each baton of cheese with a slice of the *salami*. Place on a *polenta crostini*. Repeat until all *salami* and cheese are wrapped. Place on the baking tray, sprinkle with rosemary, and cook until the cheese is starting to melt. Remove from the oven, and let cool a little before serving.

Ciauredda

Spicy sautéed vegetable crostini

serves 4

1 onion, thinly sliced

2 peppers, red or
yellow, de-seeded
and sliced into strips

2 tbsp olive oil, plus
extra for drizzling

2 ripe tomatoes,
blanched,
de-seeded, and
skinned

1 large eggplant,
peeled and cut into
tiny dice

2 medium-sized
potatoes, peeled
and cubed

salt

½–2 tsp dried red
chillies, crushed

This dish is very typical of the simple, delicious and very spicy hot specialities of this region. Delicious and as fiery as you wish to make it!

Fry the onion and the pepper together gently in a pan with the olive oil until softened.

Add the peeled and de-seeded tomatoes with the eggplant and potatoes. Stir and season with salt and continue to cook until the potatoes and eggplant are soft and cooked through, adding the chillies a few minutes before the end of the cooking time.

Serve drizzled with a little olive oil as a topping for *crostini* or as a filling for little pastry shells.

Right: Capocolle di Basilicata e caciocavallo

CALABRIA

Calabria is the southernmost region of the country; the toe of the boot, traditionally said to be kicking Sicily away into the sea. Only about two miles separate the mainland from Sicily, but the regions are very different. The landscape changes at every turn, producing an endless, stunning contrast of mountain and sea views.

At the heart of Calabria is the Sila, rolling hills covered in natural woodland of oak, beech, and chestnut trees, known as *Il Bosco d'Italia*—The Wood of Italy.

Mountain cooking and food are very much a part of the local cuisine, with wonderful cheeses and a range of cured pork products, such as the spicy soft sausage called *'nduja*. Calabrian cuisine is among the most flavorful Italy has to offer—an abundance of seafood and fantastic vegetables, especially eggplant, strawberries, onions, and peppers. The most commonly used local fish are swordfish and tuna, which are mainly caught on the western coast. *Stoccafisso*, air-dried salt cod, is also very popular.

The tradition of sheep farming in this area provides many of Calabria's lamb dishes and many sheep's milk cheeses.

Peppers here grow huge, dense, and sweeter than anywhere else. Chili peppers are a vital ingredient and are used with everything from cured meats to pasta. Figs, chestnuts, and almonds are mainly used in desserts like *fichi ripieni* (stuffed figs), a specialty of Cosenza that tops dried figs with cocoa, almonds, and other nuts. These few ingredients are essential to local cooking and form the basis of many dishes.

Calabrian cooking strikes a good balance between its many meat-based dishes, which feature pork, lamb, goat, and mutton, its varied and imaginative use of vegetables (especially peppers and eggplant), and its fish and seafood, all flavored with fragrant mountain herbs and chili.

Perhaps one of the most obvious dishes to sum up the Calabrian philosophy of food is their *caviale dei poveri*, poor man's caviar, made by packing herring roe in oil and flavoring it with hot chili peppers. The region boasts a rich, frugal peasant tradition that uses simple ingredients to make fabulous food.

Calabrians have traditionally placed a great emphasis on preserving food, partly because the heat and dry climate of the mountains inland make crop failure a distinct possibility. People plan ahead, bottling vegetables and meats in oil, salting meat, and curing fish—especially swordfish and tuna.

Calabrian cooking is not refined, nor is it rich in ingredients, but it is very substantial and infused with intense flavors and aromas—chili pepper, mint, garlic, tomatoes, peppers, eggplant, and the famous red onions of Tropea. Pork, bread (the local version is called *pitta*), the filling dried durum wheat pasta, and fish are the key culinary components of this region.

Right: A platter of authentic salami cicchetti

Involtini di melanzane

Stuffed eggplant rolls

serves 4

2 eggplants, thinly
   sliced, sprinkled
   with salt, and left to
   purge in a colander
   in the sink for 1 hour

6 tbsp olive oil, plus
   a little extra

1½ cups fresh
   bread crumbs

3 tbsp salted capers,
   rinsed

4 tbsp chopped green
   or black olives

2 tsp dried oregano

½ tsp dried, crushed
   chili pepper

The Calabrian table is never complete without at least one dish of eggplant. This is one of my favorites: a simple recipe to which you can add more or less anything that takes your fancy and that works really well with eggplant.

Preheat the oven to 375°F. Rinse and dry the eggplant, then brush with olive oil on both sides and arrange in a single layer on baking trays. Bake until soft, about 10 minutes. Remove from the oven and cool.

Meanwhile, mix the bread crumbs with the capers, olives, oregano, and chili, then add all of the remaining olive oil to make a soft and squidgy mixture.

Use this to fill each eggplant slice, rolling each slice up around a spoonful of filling and sealing closed with a toothpick.

Return the eggplant rolls to the oven for a further five to 10 minutes, then remove them from the oven. Slice them in half, discarding the toothpick, and serve warm.

Pomodorini farciti

Stuffed tomatoes

serves 4

16 large cherry
   tomatoes

1 large pinch of salt

1 small can best-
   quality tuna in
   olive oil

2 small hard-boiled
   eggs, peeled and
   finely chopped

1 tbsp finely chopped
   capers, rinsed and
   dried

2 tbsp finely chopped
   stoned green olives

1 heaped tsp
   anchovy paste

2 tbsp mayonnaise

1 tsp lemon juice

8 anchovy fillets,
   halved

This is a bit of an old-fashioned recipe, but still a great favorite and very easy to make. The addition of the anchovies gives it a grown-up twist.

Slice the tops off all the cherry tomatoes and use a teaspoon to carefully scoop out the seeds. Sprinkle each tomato with a little salt and turn them upside down in a colander or a cooling rack placed over a tray to drain.

Chop the tomato tops finely and set aside.

Drain the tuna, reserving the oil. Flake the fish with a fork and mix it with the eggs, tomato tops, capers, and olives. Add a little of the reserved oil to moisten if required.

Mix the anchovy paste with the mayonnaise and lemon juice, then mix this in with the tuna mixture. Fill each tomato to the top with the mixture and place a halved anchovy fillet on the top to serve. Chill until required, but do not serve ice-cold.

Left: Pomodorini farciti

Olive nere fritte

Pan-fried black olives

serves 4

2 garlic cloves, lightly
  crushed

4 tbsp olive oil

4 heaped tbsp dried
  black olives, stoned

2 tsp chili flakes

sea salt

Very typical of Calabria, this is a delicious way of serving black olives. Fried in olive oil and spiced up with garlic and chili, they make a wonderful snack with something cold like iced vodka or very cold and extremely dry white wine.

Put the garlic and oil into a frying pan and heat until the garlic is pungent. Add the olives and toss several times in the garlic and oil for about five minutes, then sprinkle with the chili and salt.

Leave the olives to stand for two minutes before serving hot or at room temperature.

Pizzette al salame piccante

Mini pizzas with spicy salami

serves 8

- 1 quantity basic pizza dough (see page 128)
- 5 tbsp extra virgin olive oil
- 2 tbsp coarse semolina
- ½ cup best-quality bottled tomato paste
- 6 oz fresh mozzarella, cubed
- 6 oz finely sliced Calabrian spicy salami, chopped
- 20 stoned dried black olives
- 2 tsp dried oregano

In this region, where cured pork and chili pepper form such a powerful gastronomic allegiance, it is almost inevitable that they should find their way on top of the local version of *pizza*. You can of course make one big *pizza* to cut into wedges, but little *pizzas* make great *canapés* in just two easy bites.

Preheat oven to 375°F. Form the dough into about 20 small, thin disks, using a little oil and water on your hands to help you shape them evenly. Lay them onto several oiled and *semolina*-scattered baking trays, well spaced apart.

Top each one with a tiny drizzle of olive oil, a little *passata*, a little *mozzarella*, a little chopped *salami*, and finally, one olive.

Finish off with a final drizzle of oil and bake for about eight minutes. Serve warm, dusted with dried oregano at the last moment.

Pitta di ricotta

Calabrian ricotta pizza

serves 4

3 tbsp olive oil

13 oz basic pizza dough (see below)

3 tbsp polenta or semolina

7 oz fresh ricotta

4 oz soppressata (Calabrian salami), cut into strips

2 hard-boiled eggs, peeled and finely sliced

1 heaped tbsp chopped flat-leaf parsley

2 tbsp pork fat or lard (optional)

salt and black pepper

½ tsp chili flakes

The word *pitta*, in several parts of Italy but especially Calabria, signifies a flat, flavored bread. There is a great use of pork fat in this region where the pig is king of meat products. You can leave it out of this recipe altogether if you wish, though it is traditional and very tasty.

Preheat the oven to 375°F. Knead half the oil into the dough very thoroughly and use the remaining oil to grease a 12-inch diameter shallow round baking tray.

Divide the dough into two portions, one a bit larger than the other, and roll out both thinly on a surface lightly coated with *polenta* or *semolina* to prevent sticking. Use the larger piece of dough to line the bottom and sides of the baking tray. Cover the dough with the *ricotta*, *soppressata*, eggs, flat-leaf parsley, and pork fat or lard if desired, distributing the ingredients evenly.

Finally, sprinkle with salt, pepper, and chili and cover with the remaining rolled-out dough. Seal the edges carefully, using a little cold water if necessary to help create a tight seal, and coat the top with olive oil or melted pork fat. Poke a few holes in the top with the tines of a fork to let out steam and prevent it from bursting. Bake for about 40 minutes and serve warm in small wedges.

Basic pizza dough

Makes 4 small or 2 large pizza bases

2½–3 cups all-purpose flour, plus extra for dusting

1 cherry-sized lump of fresh yeast or 1½ tsp dried yeast or 1 package easy-bake yeast

⅛ cup each very warm water and milk, mixed together

½ tsp salt

2 tbsp olive oil

tepid water, to add to the dough

2–3 tbsp semolina, for brushing over the base

The dough is your first step towards making an authentic Italian pizza. Topping possibilities are endless.

Pile the flour onto the counter and make a hollow in the center. If using fresh yeast, mix the yeast with the milk and water mixture until dissolved, wait for it to become foamy, then pour this into the hollow in the flour. Easy-bake yeast can just be added to the flour without dilution.

Add the salt and half of the oil and knead everything together thoroughly for 10 to 15 minutes until the dough is smooth and elastic. You will need to add a little more liquid or even more flour until you get the texture quite right. The dough must not feel at all tacky or sticky at the end of the kneading process and should come away from the surface and from your hands quite easily.

Use the remaining oil to grease a clean bowl. Transfer the dough into the bowl, cover snugly with a clean cloth or a sheet of lightly oiled plastic wrap and put in a warm place for about 90 minutes to two hours until it has doubled in size. Take the dough out of the bowl and knead it briefly, then use as required.

Right: Pitta di ricotta

Freselle alla Calabrese al pomodoro

Freselle with tomatoes

serves 4

4 freselle

2 tbsp cold water

2 tbsp white wine vinegar

5 ripe but firm tomatoes, calyxes removed and cubed

handful of basil leaves, torn

¼ cup extra virgin olive oil

salt

Freselle are round, hard, and dry, a cross between a biscuit and a piece of very stale, lightly toasted bread, but shaped like a flattened donut. In Calabria, as in other parts of southern Italy, they are much loved and form part of substantial salads or an easy snack. I find they are also useful as a base for very rustic and extremely tasty *canapés*. Feel free to add olives, flaked tuna, capers, or seafood to this basic recipe, or add dried oregano and finely chopped onions to the tomatoes instead of the basil.

Lay the *freselle* onto a platter and sprinkle with the water and vinegar to soften them just enough to be able to roughly cut them without shattering them.

Mix the cubed tomatoes, basil, and oil, and season with salt. Spoon this mixture over the *freselle*.

Leave to stand a few minutes to allow the flavors to permeate the *freselle*, then cut into rough pieces to serve with drinks.

APULIA

Apulia is the heel of Italy's boot; the hottest and driest of all the regions, with a long and very beautiful coastline. Inland lies Il Tavoliere, Italy's largest peninsular plain, bordered by Apulia's only two rivers. This is florid countryside, producing a glorious abundance: Italy's best wheat—providing the pasta that reigns supreme; huge black and green olives that find their way into many dishes; almonds, hazelnuts, walnuts, and all manner of vegetables; fantastic olive oil, wine, fruit—all these spill off the colorful market stalls in the streets and *piazzas* of San Severo, Cerignola, Lucera, or Trinitapoli. This is a timeless place, where very old habits are certainly not dead.

Pugliese cooking celebrates the region's golden wheat fields, the plentiful olive groves of enormous trees, the rippling vineyards, and the close proximity to both the Adriatic and the Ionian seas. The region's dry, hot climate makes it ideal for growing *grano duro*, or durum wheat—accounting for the superior, irresistible taste of its bread and pasta—and producing world-renowned olive oil. Fava beans, tomatoes, eggplant, broccoli, and zucchini are just a few of the vegetables cultivated in the region's rich, fertile soil.

On the Tavoliere, Apulia cultivates most types of wheat, but durum wheat is the main crop, as it has been for centuries. Dried pasta, such as *spaghetti*, *maccheroni*, or *penne*, is made from durum wheat. Durum comes from the Latin word *durus*, meaning "hard." This wheat's density, combined with a high protein content and its gluten strength, make this the best for producing dried pasta, providing a consistent cooking quality. Whether it's the appetizing aroma of a steaming bowl of the local *orecchiette* pasta or the warm, sweet aroma of the bread of Altamura, the Pugliesi know how to draw magic from their bounty of wheat.

This region's olive oil is one of the finest in the world. Olive oil and table olives are one of the main agricultural products of this region, which accounts for 40 percent of Italy's olive oil.

Pasta and bread play a fundamental role in Pugliese cuisine—and *Pane di Altamura* is the best example of this skill. This wonderful sourdough bread, made only with durum wheat flour harvested on the Alta Murgia near Bari, natural yeast, water, and salt, is shaped into enormous round loaves and baked in ovens fired by oak wood.

Seafood is also very popular in this region, especially in the area of Bari where the locals traditionally enjoy eating it raw, fresh from the sea. Apulia gives Italy much of her fish, as fishing is an important industry all along this long coast. Mussels and oysters are cultivated in the two seas at Taranto, and lobsters, scampi, prawns, and squid are all caught locally.

Special occasions, such as Christmas or Easter, are celebrated with special sweetmeats or desserts in this region, most of them using both the local honey and locally grown almonds to make traditional, time-honored Pugliese specialties such as *Carteddate, Mustazzeuli, Copate,* or the famously named biscuits known as *Dita D'Apostoli,* (Apostles' fingers).

Right: Fresh mackerel and shrimp at the fish market in Chioggia

Panzerotti al tonno

Tuna parcels

serves 4

5 tbsp extra virgin
olive oil

2 onions, peeled and
sliced thinly

¾ cup black olives,
stoned and chopped

2 tsp rinsed and
chopped capers

10 cherry tomatoes,
quartered

1 green pepper,
deseeded and cubed

1 tsp dried oregano

8 oz best-quality
canned tuna in olive
oil, drained and
flaked

salt

5 tbsp freshly grated
pecorino

1 quantity basic bread
dough

flour, for dusting

These tasty little parcels are really simple to make and are perfect for parties as they can be made ahead and then baked at the last minute. Make sure you use really good-quality canned tuna in olive oil—it really is worth it!

Heat half the oil in a frying pan over a medium heat and cook the onion without browning, for about 10 minutes, adding a little water if necessary.

Add the olives, capers, cherry tomatoes, green pepper, and oregano to the onions and stir. Cook together for about 10 minutes, then remove from the heat and add the tuna. Stir, adjust seasoning with salt, and leave to cool. Once cooled, stir in the *pecorino*.

Roll out the bread dough on a floured surface to a thickness of about one-quarter inch and cut into large circles—about two inches diameter.

Place a teaspoonful of the filling on one half of each circle, fold each one over to seal the filling inside, and press the edges closed tightly using the tines of a fork.

Oil and flour a large baking tray. Preheat the oven to 375°F. Brush the *panzerotti* with the remaining oil and arrange on the baking tray. Bake for about 15 to 20 minutes or until golden brown, and serve hot.

Ostriche alla cipolle alla Leccese

Oysters in the Lecce style

serves 8

16 fresh, live oysters

2 onions, finely
chopped

3 tbsp extra virgin
olive oil

5 tbsp dry white wine

¼ cup heavy cream

salt and ground white
pepper

This is a wonderful way of serving oysters and is a recipe from the beautiful old city of Lecce, in the far south of the region.

Shuck the oysters and carefully remove the mollusk from the shell. Drop the oysters into a bowl of cold water and leave to stand. Wash 16 of the empty half-shells carefully.

Fry the onions very gently in the olive oil until softened but not browned.

Drain the oysters and add them to the onions. Cook them gently for about one minute, turning them over carefully. Add the wine and cook for a further three to four minutes, then stir in the cream and season with salt and white pepper. Stir gently and allow to just thicken, then remove from the heat. Preheat the oven to 375°F.

Transfer one oyster back into each clean half-shell and cover with the sauce and onions. Arrange the oysters on a baking tray and bake in the oven for five minutes before serving.

Right: Ostriche alla cipolle alla leccese

Pizzelle di cozze
e basilico

Mussels with basil on crusty bread

serves 8

1³/₄ lb fresh live
    mussels

12 slices of altamura
    bread or crusty
    bread

6 tbsp basic tomato
    sauce (see page 138)

4 tbsp extra virgin
    olive oil

salt

1 handful of fresh
    basil leaves

Everybody in Apulia is mad about seafood, and there are countless delicious recipes for making the most of all the bounty that the long coastline has to offer. Also deservedly famous is the deliciously tasty bread of Altamura. If you can find it, it will make this recipe really special, but any good-quality crusty bread will also work well.

Clean and wash all the mussels and place then in a large pot over high heat. Steam, covered, for about five to eight minutes, shaking the pot frequently to encourage them all to open.

Remove the pot from the heat and leave to cool until easy to handle, then remove all the mollusks from their shells.

Oil a baking tray and lay the bread in it. Preheat the oven to 400°F. Spread each slice of bread with tomato sauce and cover with shelled mussels, drizzle with oil, sprinkle with salt, and place in the oven for 10 minutes. Remove from the oven, sprinkle with the basil, and serve at once.

Il sugo di pomodoro all'aglio

Basic tomato sauce with garlic

serves 4

4 tbsp richly flavored extra virgin olive oil

3 garlic cloves, smashed

2 cups passata

salt and black pepper

1 handful of fresh herbs, such as basil, parsley, or oregano, chopped

Passata is simply fresh tomatoes pushed through a sieve to liquefy them, and remove the seeds and skins. It can be bought at grocery stores, or ordered online. Or, make your own if you grow tomatoes.

Fry the garlic very gently with the olive oil in a heavy-bottomed pot or frying pan. Don't let the garlic color or it will give a bitter flavor to the whole sauce. If the garlic goes brown, discard at once, wipe out the pan, and start again.

When the garlic is pungent, remove it and pour in the *passata*, and stir carefully. Simmer over a medium heat for about 10 minutes or until the sauce is glossy and thick. Season to taste, and cover.

Take off the heat and keep warm, adding the herbs as you prefer.

Rotolini di cozze

Pancake rolls with mussels

serves 8

14 oz fresh, live mussels

4 tbsp extra virgin olive oil

16 small, fresh anchovies

1½ cups all-purpose flour, plus extra for dusting

1 cup fresh ricotta

salt

2 oz pecorino shavings

1 egg, beaten

Another delicious recipe for mussels from the city of Lecce, combining them with *ricotta* and *pecorino*, with the added fishy flavor of anchovies.

Clean and wash the mussels carefully, then put them into a large pot with a tablespoon of oil and cover. Place the pot over a lively heat for about five to eight minutes, shaking the pot frequently to encourage all the mussels to open up.

Remove from the heat and leave to cool until easy to handle, then remove all the mollusks from the shells and discard the shells. Clean and gut the anchovies and remove the bones. Wash and set aside.

Blend the flour with the *ricotta*, three-quarters of the remaining oil, and a pinch of salt. Leave the resulting dough to rest for about 30 minutes. Preheat the oven to 375°F and thoroughly oil a shallow baking dish.

Roll the rested dough out on a floured surface and cut into rectangles—approximately 2 x 3 inches. Place a couple of mussels, one anchovy fillet, and a few *pecorino* shavings on each rectangle and season with salt.

Roll all the rectangles up tightly and arrange them neatly in the baking dish. Brush them with the beaten egg and bake in the preheated oven for about 10 minutes or until golden brown. Remove from the oven, slice in half, arrange on a dish, and serve at once.

Right: Il sugo di pomodoro all'aglio

Overleaf: Backstreets of Monte Sant'Angelo, in the Foggia province

CAMPANIA

Italian food would not be the same without Campania's ubiquitous *spaghetti* topped with *la pommarola*, their famous tomato sauce. Campania is also the birthplace of *pizza*, where the world's first pizzeria started on the streets of Naples. The volcanic soils of Campania grow what may possibly be the best produce in the whole of Italy, including tomatoes, peaches, grapes, apricots, figs, oranges, and lemons. Campania's most famous cheese is the *mozzarella di bufala*, made from the precious milk of local water buffalos. Other popular cheeses include *pecorino*, *provolone*, *caciocavallo*, *scamorza*, and *ricotta* (both cow and buffalo versions). Seafood is a staple along Campania's coastline with fish fried, octopus, cuttlefish, squid, clams, and mussels featuring heavily.

To many foreigners Italian cuisine actually means Neapolitan cooking. Many of the Italian immigrants to other parts of Europe and the United States came from the Campanian city of Naples and its environs. The wonderful food of this region has traveled around the world. When they open restaurants in new countries, Neapolitans naturally serve the food they know best.

The complex history of this region explains the diversity of its cuisine. The French and Spanish influenced the dishes eaten by the rich, dishes that were showy and striking in appearance although often not necessarily nourishing. The cuisine of the poor, actually the population at large, consisted of plenty of vegetables and dairy, where meat is almost nonexistent and fish reserved for feasts.

At the center of this cuisine sits the tomato. Colorful, bursting with vitamins, and easily united with a thousand other flavors, the tomato is a quintessential part of the local cooking. A relatively recent arrival: it came to Europe (and Italy) from Peru or Mexico after the discovery of America, only to be entirely ignored for two centuries. The tomato was mentioned for the first time in 1743 in a song, but it is only between the end of the eighteenth and the beginning of the nineteenth century that it became a common ingredient and its cultivation spread.

The *pizza*, that most famous creation of Neapolitan cuisine, has very ancient origins, older than the arrival of the tomato. In fact, the original *pizza* would have been made without tomato sauce. But the *pizza* we know and love today, coated with tomato paste, sizzling and cheerful as no other type of food is, is only just over two hundred years old.

While pasta was not invented in Naples, it has certainly reached the highest level of perfection there. At Gragnano, only a few miles from the capital city of the region, it was first discovered how to dry pasta for preservation, thus making way for its industrial production. Since raw durum wheat is very difficult to mix and process, Neapolitans rely on mass-produced pasta, and do not in the slightest believe (as in other regions) that to be good, pasta must be homemade. In Naples, pasta is extraordinary for its quality, for being correctly cooked to *al dente*, and for its wonderful dressings and sauces.

Neapolitan gastronomy also includes a series of dishes that go back to the traditions of the courts or to the genuine French-inspired "school" that was followed by a group of noble families especially in the 1800s. Recipes were created in which refined French contributions were combined with typically Neapolitan ingredients and customs. This resulted in very elaborate and spectacular inventions. The mistress of the house would entrust the management and preparation of their feasts to expert French chefs who were to become famous for their art.

The most classic cakes and desserts of Naples are the ice creams, *baba*, *spumoni*, *sfogliatelle*, *taralli*, and the magnificent *pastiera* cake, eaten from Epiphany to Easter, with fresh *ricotta* and orange blossom water, cinnamon, and candied fruit. Food in Naples is a joyful experience. From the *friggi e mangia* ("fry and eat") kiosks to the many products of the local *rosticceria* (delicatessen) to the various *passatempi* ("pass-times"), street food is on sale in the park kiosks or roadside stands at any time during the day. It consists of seafood, small *pizzas*, tarts, or fritters. Naples and Campania always extravagantly display a legendary culinary tradition that stretches back thousands of years.

Right: A bàcaro's generous selection of spirits in Borgo Marinaro, Naples

Calzoncini

Mini calzoni

**makes
about 10**

1 quantity basic pizza
  dough (see page 128)

flour, for dusting

6 tbsp extra virgin
  olive oil

3 tbsp polenta or
  coarse semolina

6 heaped tbsp ricotta

10 thin slices of
  salami, finely
  chopped

10 sun-dried
  tomatoes in oil,
  drained and halved

The Italian word *calzoni* means "trousers," and *calzoncini* means "shorts"! These are basically little stuffed pizzas.

Preheat the oven to 400°F. Roll the dough out onto a floured surface and cut it into about 10 small disks; you can re-knead and re-roll the scraps as you go along.

  Oil a baking tray (or several) and sprinkle with the *polenta* or *semolina*.

  Place a teaspoon of *ricotta*, a teaspoon of chopped *salami*, and half a sun-dried tomato on each disk, and then fold them in half to seal, using the tines of a fork to crimp a tight seal around the open edge.

  Brush with the remaining olive oil and bake for about 10 minutes or until they are golden brown. Serve hot.

Piccolo fritto misto di pesce

Mini fritto misto of fish

serves 12

4¼ cups cheap olive
  oil

6 oz squid

6 oz whitebait

16 large raw shrimp,
  with tail shells left on

½ cup all-purpose
  flour, seasoned with
  salt and pepper

2 lemons, cut into 12
  wedges, to serve

The art of frying food is hugely popular in Campania. In Naples people tend to do their frying out on a balcony over a single gas ring to prevent the house filling with the smell of frying fish. The secret is to have clean, hot oil and to serve the *fritto* quickly so it retains all its special crispiness.

Cut the squid pouches across into rings and separate the tentacles into pairs.

  Toss the seafood, a few pieces at a time, in the seasoned flour to cover lightly. Heat a wok or large, heavy-based pan containing the oil. When it starts to smoke, drop a crust of bread in. If the oil starts to froth around the bread and the bread turns golden, it is ready and you can start frying the seafood in batches for one minute, until crisp and golden.

  Use a slotted spoon to lift the seafood onto a paper towel-lined baking tray to drain and keep warm in the oven while you cook the rest.

  When all the seafood is cooked, serve at once with lemon wedges.

Right: Piccolo fritto misto di pesce

Spiedini di scamorza

Scamorza skewers

makes 4

14 oz smoked
  scamorza

¼ cup olive oil

salt and black pepper

7 oz crusty bread,
  sliced

4 thin slices smoked
  pancetta, cut into
  quarters

This delicious dish comes from the town of Caserta, in the heart of the cheese-making area where *mozzarella* in all forms rules!

Slice the *scamorza* and dress it lightly with olive oil and salt and pepper.

Grill the bread until crisp and browned, then cut it into cubes. Preheat the oven to 300°F.

Slide the cubes of bread, slices of *scamorza*, and slices of *pancetta* onto little skewers, alternating the ingredients until you have used them all.

Use any remaining oil to grease a baking tray. Lay the skewers onto the baking tray and place in the oven to heat through and lightly melt the cheese for about 10 minutes before serving.

Casatiello

Neapolitan cheese loaf

serves 12

3¼ cups all-purpose
  flour, plus extra for
  dusting

7 oz pork lard or ¾ cup
  olive oil

salt and black pepper

1½ oz fresh yeast

1 oz pecorino romano,
  grated

2 oz parmesan, grated

4 eggs

This great Neapolitan classic is delicious served with a selection of cured meats such as a soft and spicy *salami*. Omit the eggs if you prefer not to shell them after the bread is baked.

Tip the flour onto the work surface, make a hollow in the center, and add half the lard or oil and a generous pinch of salt and pepper. Place the yeast in a cup of warm water and mix until the yeast is melted and frothy. Leave to stand for 10 minutes until it is activated, then add this mixture to the flour. Knead everything together energetically for 15 minutes until you have a smooth and elastic ball of dough. Add more water if necessary.

Place the dough in an oiled bowl and leave to rise in a warm place, covered with a cloth or a sheet of oiled plastic wrap for two hours.

When the dough has risen, knead it briefly again, then roll it out onto a floured surface into a wide, thick rectangle. Spread half the remaining lard or drizzle half the remaining oil all over the middle of the rectangle.

Sprinkle the dough with half the cheeses and add plenty of pepper. Fold it in half and repeat with the remaining cheese and more pepper. Shape into a long sausage and place in a ring mold, well greased with lard or oil. Leave to rise for a further two hours.

Carefully wash and dry the four eggs, taking care not to crack them. Preheat the oven to 300°F. Once the dough has risen again, carefully push the whole eggs into the surface of the *casatiello* in four different places and bake in the oven for about one hour. Remove from the oven and cool before removing from the ring mold and slicing to serve, shelling the eggs as necessary.

Left: Spiedini di scamorza

Uova stracciate alla Napoletana

Neapolitan scrambled eggs

serves 12

8 tbsp unsalted butter

8 large anchovy fillets

4 oz canned tomatoes,
or fresh tomatoes,
peeled, chopped,
and deseeded

4 oz mozzarella, cubed

2 tsp dried oregano

salt and black pepper

8 large eggs, beaten

As a really tasty way of scrambling eggs, this will cheer up even the most jaded palate. Serve on little rounds of toast as a *canapé* or in small cups with a teaspoon.

Melt the butter in a large pan and add the anchovies. Cook gently until the anchovies have melted completely.

Stir in the tomatoes and simmer for 20 minutes.

Add the *mozzarella*, oregano, salt, and pepper, and stir together, then pour in the beaten eggs and cook until just set. Serve at once.

LAZIO

Lazio's food is not for the fainthearted or the squeamish, typified as it is by offal dishes and plenty of olive oil and garlic. This is largely strong and vigorous food, not designed for those with small appetites. It is food for hardworking people and warriors. All of this is reflected fully in the tastes, smells, and textures of Lazio's favorite dishes.

The traditional cooking of Lazio reflects the meals of shepherds and farmers, made from a few ingredients and prepared simply. It's no surprise to find that tender, milk-fed lamb (*abbacchio*) is a favorite dish, usually baked and served with seasonal vegetables. The countryside surrounding Rome is known as La Campagna Romana, and has for thousands of years been used as a vast vegetable and fruit market for the city.

When you reach Rome, the cuisine emerges as a savory medley, incorporating the traditions of Lazio with an amalgam of flavors, textures, and ingredients from outlying areas, and also from the Jewish quarter of the city. Rome, the regional capital of Lazio, is also the capital city of Italy. Though officially part of Central Italy, Roman cuisine has characteristics that link it much more strongly with the south.

Roman cooking is traditionally dominated by the earthy cuisine of the working classes, with a little influence from the city's centuries-old Jewish population thrown in. Although you'll find all sorts of pasta served in Roman restaurants, *spaghetti* is common, as is the local specialty of *bucatini* or thick-cut *spaghetti* (sometimes called *tonarelli*), as they stand up well to the coarse, gutsy sauces the Romans prefer: *aglio e olio* (garlic and oil),

cacio e pepe (*pecorino* and black pepper), *alla carbonara* (with beaten eggs, cubes of pan-fried *guanciale*—cured pork jowl—or bacon, and *pecorino* or *parmesan*), and *alle vongole* (with baby clams).

Fish is an integral, though usually pricey, part of Roman cuisine, and features most frequently as salt cod, *baccala'*, which is best eaten Jewish-style: deep-fried.

Offal is also key, and although it has been ousted from many of the more refined city-center restaurants, you'll still find it on the menus of more traditional places, especially those in Testaccio. Most favored is *pajata*, the intestines of an unweaned calf, but you'll also find *lingua* (tongue), *rognone* (kidney), *milza* (spleen)—delicious as a *pâté* on toasted bread, and *trippa* (tripe). Look out too for *coda alla vaccinara*, oxtail stewed in a rich sauce of tomato and celery; *testerelle d'abbacchio*, lamb's head baked in the oven with herbs and oil; and *coratella*, lamb's heart, liver, lungs, and spleen cooked in olive oil with lots of black pepper and onions. More conventional meat dishes include the aforementioned *abbacchio*, milk-fed lamb roasted to melting tenderness with rosemary, sage, and garlic; *scottadito*, grilled lamb chops eaten with the fingers; and *saltimbocca alla Romana*, thin slices of veal cooked with a slice of *prosciutto* and sage on top.

Artichokes (*carciofi*) are the quintessential Roman vegetable, served *alla Romana* (stuffed with garlic and Roman mint and then baked or braised) and "*alla giudea*"—flattened out and then deep-fried in olive oil.

Lazio's wine comes mainly from the Castelli Romani (most famously from Frascati) to the south, and from around Montefiascone (Est! Est!! Est!!!) in the north.

Right: The Spanish Steps in front of the Trinità dei Monti, Rome

Pinzimonio

Raw vegetable and olive oil dip

serves 4

1 large fennel bulb

1 carrot

1 zucchini

4 scallions

1¼ cups very best-
    quality extra virgin
    olive oil

salt and black pepper

This classic Roman *antipasto* or snack is simplicity itself to prepare, but relies entirely on the quality of the oil and the vegetables for success.

Remove all the outer tough layers from the fennel, then cut the tender center into eight equal segments.

Peel and halve the carrot lengthwise, then cut it into shorter sticks. Wash and cut the ends off the zucchini, then halve it and cut into sticks the same size as the carrots. Trim the scallions, wash, and halve lengthwise.

Mix the oil with salt and pepper to taste, then pour into a small serving bowl. Surround with the crisp, raw vegetables, and serve.

Fegato ripieno all'antica Roma

Stuffed liver in the ancient Roman style

serves 4

1 large onion

8 large, ripe figs

4 large slices thickly
    cut calves' liver

5 tbsp extra virgin
    olive oil

¾ cup dry white wine

2 tbsp runny honey

salt and black pepper

This is a very old dish, still cooked today in much the same way it would have been enjoyed in ancient Roman times.

Chop the onion coarsely and cut the figs into small pieces. Trim the liver, removing any gristle or skin, and wrap each slice around an equal quantity of fig pieces. Tie the liver slices securely with cook's string.

Fry the onion gently in a pan with the oil until softened, then add the liver rolls and turn them in the onion and oil to brown them all over, for about four minutes.

Mix the wine and the honey together and pour over the liver rolls. Cook for a further two minutes, basting with the wine and honey. Season to taste.

Remove from the pan, allow to cool for two minutes, then remove the string, cut into rounds, and serve, drizzled with the juices from the pan.

Right: Pinzimonio

Supplì alla Romana

Roman rice fritters

serves 4, or
more if made
smaller

1 onion, finely
chopped

1 carrot, finely
chopped

1 celery stick, finely
chopped

3 tbsp olive oil

4 oz ground beef

4 tbsp red wine

½ cup passata

salt and black pepper

1½ cups arborio or
carnaroli rice

4 cups hot vegetable
stock

2 eggs

7 oz mozzarella

1 cup dried bread
crumbs

2 cups sunflower oil

These are not like the Sicilian *arancini*, due to their different shape. They are long and oval like a *croquette*, and they contain a meaty tomato sauce, in which the rice is cooked. The secret of a real *suppli* is that it is a bright, vivid red on the inside, thanks to the sauce.

Fry the onion, carrot, and celery in the oil until softened, then add the beef and cook it thoroughly until browned all over. Add the red wine, boil off the alcohol for two minutes, then add the *passata* and stir together. Season with salt and pepper and simmer for 15 to 30 minutes, then add all of the rice. Gradually add the stock, and cook, stirring, until the rice is completely cooked. Remove the pan from the heat, transfer to a wide, shallow tray and leave to cool completely.

Beat the eggs in a wide, shallow bowl and set aside. Cut the *mozzarella* into small cubes. Spread the bread crumbs onto a wide, shallow tray. Pour the oil into a wide pan and set it over a low heat to begin to warm up.

Take a handful of the cooked rice, make a hollow, and push a cube of *mozzarella* into it. Cover with more rice and shape into a long *croquette* shape.

Roll in the beaten egg, and then in the bread crumbs, ensuring the bread crumbs are solidly stuck on and that the *suppli* is firmly shaped and will hold together when dropped into the hot oil.

Fry all the *suppli* in the hot oil for about five minutes, or until crisp and golden. Drain on paper towels and serve piping hot.

Frittelle di gamberetti

Shrimp fritters

serves 6

1 lb small shrimp, peeled

1½ cups chickpea flour

1 tbsp finely chopped flat-leaf parsley

3 scallions, finely chopped

¼ tsp paprika

salt

olive oil, for deep frying

These are similar to the Spanish *tortillitas de camarones*, which is not surprising given Rome's history as a busy shipping port. They have an earthy flavor due to the chickpea flour, but you can substitute all-purpose flour if you can't get hold of this.

Cover the shrimp with water and bring to a boil over high heat. As soon as the water starts to boil, lift out the shrimp with a slotted spoon and set aside. Scoop out one cup cooking water and let cool. Discard remaining water. When the shrimp are cool, cover and refrigerate.

Make the batter by combining flour, parsley, scallions, and paprika in a bowl. Add a pinch of salt and the cooled cooking water and mix well. Cover and refrigerate for one hour. Mince the shrimp very finely, and add to the chilled batter. Mix well.

Pour olive oil into a heavy sauté pan to about one-inch deep, then heat until almost smoking. Add one tablespoon of batter to the oil for each fritter and, using the back of a spoon, flatten into a three-inch round. Do not crowd pan. Using a slotted spoon, lift out the fritters, holding them briefly over the pan to allow excess oil to drain, and transfer to paper towels. When all the fritters are cooked, arrange on a platter and serve immediately.

Mozzarella in carrozza

Mozzarella in a golden carriage

serves 4

8 slices white bread,
    crusts removed

1½ tsp anchovy paste

8 thick slices of
    mozzarella

black pepper

3 eggs, beaten

sunflower oil
    for deep-frying

This is quite a heavy dish, given that it is deep-fried bread and cheese, so should be served on its own or with other very light components to make up a meal. The pastry forms a lovely golden-brown casing for the melted cheese inside, like Cinderella riding to the ball in a golden coach.

Lay four slices of bread out on a board and spread each one with anchovy paste. Cover the anchovy paste with slices of *mozzarella*. Season with a little freshly milled pepper and cover with the other slices of bread. Squash these sandwiches together very firmly.

Break the eggs into a bowl, beat them thoroughly, and slide the sandwiches into the beaten eggs. Leave to soak for about 15 minutes.

Meanwhile, pour an approximately three-inch depth of sunflower oil into a wide, deep frying pan and heat until a small cube of bread, dropped onto the surface of the oil, sizzles instantly.

Fry the four sandwiches in the hot oil until crisp and golden on both sides, remove from the hot oil with a spatula, and drain very thoroughly on paper towels.

Cut into wedges or cubes to serve as a *canapé* but whatever you do, serve piping hot, perhaps with a bowl of tomato sauce offered separately for dipping.

Bruschetta con le mazzancolle

Bruschetta with langoustines

serves 4

1½ lbs langoustines,
    crayfish, or shrimp
    cooked

8 tbsp béchamel (see
    page 60)

juice of 1 small lemon

salt and black pepper

4 thick slices ciabatta
    or other crusty
    Italian bread

3 tbsp finely chopped
    flat-leaf parsley

This is simply delicious, perfect with a chilled glass of *prosecco* or *frascati*. If langoustines are not available where you live, use crayfish or jumbo shrimp instead.

Shell the langoustines, crayfish, or shrimp and remove all the flesh, discarding the shells. Chop the meat coarsely, mix with the *béchamel*, and stir in the lemon juice. Season and set aside. Toast the bread on both sides, then spread thickly with the prawn or crayfish mixture. Sprinkle with the flat-leaf parsley and serve, cut into smaller wedges if preferred.

Left: Mozzarella in carrozza

Agnello a scottadito

Grilled lamb cutlets

serves 4

8 small, lean lamb cutlets

salt and black pepper

1 garlic clove, crushed

1 rosemary sprig, chopped

3 tbsp extra virgin olive oil

The name of this dish means "burn-your-fingers" lamb; in other words, it needs to be served very hot and eaten only with the fingers!

Light the grill or heat a chargrill pan until very hot.

Meanwhile, batten the lamb cutlets lightly to flatten them slightly and even them out, and trim off any excess fat. Season the lamb generously with salt and pepper.

Mix the garlic, rosemary, and olive oil together and brush over the lamb on both sides.

Grill the lamb for about two minutes on each side before serving.

Maciotti

Hot polenta flour buns with golden raisins and rosemary

serves 4

4 cups polenta flour

2 tbsp extra virgin olive oil

2 cups golden raisins, soaked in 2 cups of water until soft

1 tsp finely chopped rosemary

2 tbsp runny honey

This is a really simple recipe, delicious served with soft, ripe *gorgonzola* and some good red wine.

Preheat the oven to 325°F. Mix the *polenta* flour with the oil, the drained, soaked golden raisins, and enough of the soaking water to make a soft dough.

Knead in the rosemary and the honey and then shape into fist-sized balls. Flatten the top of each one very slightly and then bake for about an hour, or until crispy on the outside. Serve hot.

Right: Agnello a scottadito

SICILY

With such a rich and diverse history, Sicily promises an unparalleled culinary tour, and no single dish or flavor alone can epitomize its cooking. Phoenicians, Greeks, Romans, Arabs, Normans, Spaniards, and the French House of Savoy have all left their mark on this glorious island and on the unique panoply of its traditional cuisine. In particular, the Arabs, who conquered the island in 827, gave Sicily the eggplant, citrus fruits, cotton, and jasmine, to mention but a few things. They are even supposed to have introduced the island to handmade pasta. Incidentally, the most famous pasta dish of Sicily is called *pasta con le sarde*, pasta with sardines, made with fresh sardines, fennel fronds, saffron, raisins, and pine nuts. It is delicious and truly reflects the extraordinary flavor combinations that are so brilliantly created on this island.

In Palermo, to the west, you can feast on Arabian-inspired vegetable couscous and roast lamb made with herbs and spices from one of the town's bustling open-air markets. Venture down to the southern coast for fish, mussels, and clams, which taste remarkably fresh because they have just been plucked from the Mediterranean.

Ice cream is also supposed to have been introduced to the island by the Arabs, and in Sicily it has almost become an obsession. Many flavors and varieties are available, including the very special *granita al caffè con panna*, a slushy iced coffee topped with whipped cream. You can even have it inside a *brioche* bun for a cooling breakfast.

Sicilians are hugely fond of *caponata*, a traditional *antipasto* made of eggplant, pine nuts, celery, olives, and capers. The recipe varies from place to place and sometimes it even includes chocolate.

No Italian kitchen would be complete without a bottle of marsala wine. Centuries ago, this cooking staple was created in the western Sicilian town of Marsala to challenge the Portuguese and Spanish monopoly on fortified wines such as madeira and sherry. Today Marsala is used all over the world to enhance the flavor of a dish or create the base of a sauce, or is enjoyed as a dessert wine.

It's virtually impossible to walk straight past a Sicilian pastry shop window, with its explosion of tantalizing colors and flavors. Among the vast array of Sicilian sweets, the place of honor definitely goes to the traditional *cassata*. Made of an enticing mixture of sponge cake, chocolate, sweetened *ricotta*, candied fruit, and nuts, the super-sweet *cassata* is usually decorated with thick icing or marzipan and covered with brightly colored candied fruits. The ever-popular *cannoli*, deep-fried pastry cylinders filled with a rich combination of sweetened *ricotta* mixed with chocolate and candied fruit, were once a treat only at Carnival time, but are now enjoyed year-round.

Frutta martorana are traditional marzipan sweets in the form of fruits and vegetables from the province of Palermo. Very realistically shaped, and colored with vegetable dyes, they are said to have originated at the Monastero di Martorano in Palermo, when nuns decorated empty fruit trees with marzipan fruit to impress an archbishop visiting at Easter. Traditionally, they are placed by children's bedsides on All Saints' Eve to commemorate and honor the dead—just one of many traditions linked to foods in Sicily.

Right: View of the Votive Temple of Christ the King belltower, Messina, Sicily

Arancini di riso con la mozzarella

Fried rice balls with mozzarella

serves 6

This recipe comes from the town of Caltanisetta.

1 onion, finely
    chopped

8 tbsp unsalted butter

1½ cups arborio or
    carnaroli rice

2 cups vegetable or
    chicken broth, kept
    hot

4 oz parmesan, grated

salt and black pepper

3 eggs

¾ cup bread crumbs

2 mozzarella balls,
    drained and cubed

4¼ cups sunflower oil

In a large frying pan, fry the onion in half the butter until it has softened, then add the rice and toast the grains, turning them for five minutes without letting them brown.

Gradually add the hot broth, one ladleful at a time, and stir constantly until the rice is cooked and the broth has been absorbed.

Stir in the rest of the butter and the *parmesan*, season with salt and pepper to taste, and leave to cool.

Beat the eggs in a shallow bowl and spread the bread crumbs onto a tray. Pour the oil into a new frying pan and warm over a low heat.

Shape the cooled *risotto* into balls the size of a small orange and make a hollow in the center with your thumb. Push a cube of *mozzarella* into the hollow and cover the indentation with more rice.

Roll the balls in your hands to shape them and make sure they are secure before rolling in the beaten eggs, then coating with the bread crumbs, and shaking off any excess.

Heat a wok or large, heavy-based pan containing the oil. When it starts to smoke, drop a crust of bread in. If the oil starts to froth around the bread and the bread turns golden, it is ready and you can start frying the balls in batches. Then drain thoroughly on paper towels to absorb any excess oil. Serve piping hot.

Capperi fritti

Deep-fried capers

serves 8

8 oz large salted capers

1 tbsp all-purpose
    flour

2 cups sunflower
    oil, for frying

This is a very simple little snack, excellent with drinks, but be sure to remove all traces of excess salt from the capers before you begin, and make sure you only use the big, fat capers such as those from the island of Pantelleria.

Soak the salted capers overnight in cold water, then rinse and dry very thoroughly. Coat them lightly in flour, using a sieve to help you.

Heat the oil until sizzling, then quickly toss in the capers and fry for just one minute, or until crisp. Remove from the oil with a slotted spoon and drain thoroughly on paper towels to absorb excess oil before serving at once.

Left: Arancini di riso con la mozzarella

Arancini di riso con la carne

Fried rice balls with meat

serves 6 to 8

1 large onion, finely
chopped

4 tbsp extra virgin
olive oil

14 oz ground beef

1¼ cups red wine

salt and black pepper

1½ cups arborio or
carnaroli rice

1¾ oz parmesan or
pecorino

3–4 tbsp unsalted
butter

4 oz ricotta

6 tbsp béchamel
sauce (see page 60)

3 eggs

1 cup dried bread
crumbs

4 cups sunflower oil,
for frying

This is the original recipe from the beautiful city of Siracusa in southeastern Sicily.

Fry the onion in the oil until softened and golden, then add the ground beef and fry until it is brown it all over. Add the red wine and burn off the alcohol for two minutes, stirring, then season with salt and pepper. Reduce the heat to the absolute minimum and leave to simmer very, very gently for 30 minutes, then remove from the heat and cool.

Bring a large pot of salted water to a boil. Add the rice and cook until tender, then drain and tip into a bowl. Add the butter and *parmesan* and mix together with two forks. Spread out the rice in a large, shallow dish to cool completely.

Mix together the cooked beef, *ricotta*, and *béchamel* sauce. Beat the eggs in a separate, wide bowl and measure the bread crumbs out onto a tray.

Take a handful of rice and shape into a ball the size of a small orange, then push a hole into the middle with your thumb. Fill the hollow with some of the beef and *ricotta* filling, then cover with more rice. Roll the ball to secure the filling and make it as round and smooth as possible. Continue until the rice and the filling have been used up.

Roll the balls in the beaten egg, then in the bread crumbs, and shake off any excess.

Heat a wok or large, heavy-based pan containing the oil. When it starts to smoke, drop a crust of bread in. If the oil starts to froth around the bread and the bread turns golden, it is ready and you can start frying the *arancini* in batches.

Drain on plenty of paper towels to remove any excess oil. Serve at once.

Polpette nella foglia di limone

Meatballs wrapped in lemon leaves

serves 4

14 oz ground veal, beef, turkey, or chicken

¾ cup dried bread crumbs

4 oz *caciocavallo* or parmesan cheese, grated

1 large egg

salt and black pepper

3 tbsp chopped flat-leaf parsley

½ wine glass cold water

24 lemon leaves, washed and dried

6 tbsp olive oil, for drizzling

1 tsp lemon zest, to serve

These little meatballs are delicious and gorgeous to look at. They also remain wonderfully moist, and the oils from the lemon leaves add a very special flavor.

Mix the meat, bread crumbs, cheese, egg, salt, pepper, and flat-leaf parsley together very thoroughly, then blend in the water gradually. Mix with your hands for a few minutes, then shape the soft mixture into small balls about the size of a large walnut and press them slightly flat with your palms.

Sandwich each ball between two lemon leaves, securing them with two wooden toothpicks. Cook them over moderate heat on a barbecue or under a grill until the leaves begin to burn slightly, turning them over after about four minutes.

Serve piled on a platter, drizzled with olive oil and sprinkled with lemon zest, warning your guests to unwrap them before eating!

Tip:

If no lemon leaves are available, fry the meatballs in 6 tbsp olive oil, or grill as above. Drain them on paper towels and sprinkle with lemon juice and grated rind before serving.

Panelle

Chickpea fritters

serves 4

2¾ cups chickpea flour

6⅓ cups water

½ tsp fine salt

black pepper

1 tsp lightly crushed fennel seeds, or 3 tbsp finely chopped fresh flat-leaf parsley

2 tbsp extra virgin olive oil

4 cups sunflower oil for deep-frying

Don't be fooled by these humble little fritters. They are irresistible and make the perfect party *cicchetti*.

Mix the flour and water together very thoroughly, season with salt and pepper, and leave to stand for about 30 minutes or longer.

Put the mixture over low heat and bring to a boil, stirring continuously and carefully until the mixture comes away from the sides of the pan. This is quite hard work but it is essential. Sprinkle the fennel seeds or parsley into the mixture toward the end of the cooking time, with about 10 minutes to go.

Once the mixture is cooked, pour it out into a lightly oiled tray. Spread it out carefully and evenly with a spatula to one-third of an inch thickness.

Allow the mixture to cool and set, then slice into about 12 small rectangles.

Heat a wok or large, heavy-based pan containing the oil. When it starts to smoke, drop a crust of bread in. If the oil starts to froth around the bread and the bread turns golden, it is ready and you can start frying the rectangles until they are crisp and hot. Serve at once.

Left: Piazza Pretoria, Palermo, Sicily

Polpettine di melanzane

Eggplant fritters

makes 24 fritters

2 lbs eggplant, thickly sliced

4 oz golden raisins

2 egg yolks

3 oz pecorino, grated

1 large pinch of dried oregano

¼ tsp nutmeg

black pepper

3 tbsp all-purpose flour

1 egg, beaten

1 cup fresh white bread crumbs

4 cups sunflower oil, for frying

Here is another delicious way to use more eggplant in your cooking, with truly mouth-watering results.

Put the eggplant into a frying pan and cover with cold, salted water. Put a heavy plate on top and leave for about 45 minutes. In a bowl, cover the golden raisins with water and let them soak for 45 minutes. Drain the eggplant slices and put them back in the frying pan with enough fresh water to cover them.

Drain the golden raisins and set aside.

Boil the eggplant for about five minutes, then drain. Squeeze out as much water as you can by hand then then chop it as finely as possible.

Put the eggplant into a bowl and add the golden raisins, egg yolks, *pecorino*, oregano, nutmeg, and plenty of black pepper. Mix everything together, then shape into little balls. Roll them first in the flour, then in the beaten egg, and then in the bread crumbs.

Heat a wok or large, heavy-based pan containing the oil. When it starts to smoke, drop a crust of bread in. If the oil starts to froth around the bread and the bread turns golden, it is ready and you can start frying the fritters in batches. Drain them on paper towels and serve hot or cold.

Alivi cunsati

Sicilian marinated olives

makes 1 serving bowl

1 lb green olives, preserved in brine

2 tbsp chopped fresh dill

4 garlic cloves, crushed

15 mint leaves

sea salt

4 oz celery, chopped

6 tbsp extra-virgin olive oil

8 tbsp red wine vinegar

½ red chili, de-seeded and finely chopped

The longer the olives are left in their marinade, the stronger the flavor they will take on, but they can be equally delicious served almost immediately after being dressed.

Drain the olives, then put them into a heavy-duty plastic bag and loosely tie closed. Place the bag on a worktop and, with a rolling pin, lightly crush the olives (it is more a matter of cracking them), then transfer the olives out of the bag and into a bowl. Add the dill, garlic, mint, and a pinch of salt, then cover with water. Let soak for a minimum of one hour or a maximum of three days. Drain, then add the celery, olive oil, and vinegar, and finally the chopped chili. Stir it all thoroughly and serve, or let stand until required.

Left: Alivi cunsati

SARDINIA

Sardinian cuisine unites the dishes from its ancient shepherding and farming traditions with those that are based on fish and seafood, adding the unmistakable aromas and flavors of the island's Mediterranean herbs.

This cuisine is strictly linked to the seasons. Its secret lies in the quality of the ingredients and the simplicity of the dishes. What emerges are dishes full of unique flavors, with each area of the island boasting its own specialties, all prepared according to their own ancient traditions and customs.

The selection of ingredients that are provided by both the land and sea mean that the choice of delicious main courses is particularly rich. Among the many celebrated meat dishes, the most well known is *porceddu*, a suckling pig cooked on a spit or *a carraxiu*, cooked in a hole in the ground, using the aromatic wood of the Mediterranean scrubland. However, there are numerous other mouth-watering dishes, such as wild boar in *cannonau* wine, and quail or chicken wrapped in myrtle leaves.

Among the many fish and seafood dishes, there is lobster prepared with citrus fruit in Alghero, with tomatoes in Bosa, grilled in Sant'Antioco, and braised with white wine in Santa Teresa di Gallura.

In Cagliari, the island's capital city, you can sample sea urchin eggs spread onto toasted bread, or *burrida*, a dish of dogfish made with walnuts and vinegar. In and around Oristano, the traditional dish is *merca*, or mullet steeped in saltwater and herbs. *Bottarga*, salted or dried mullet or tuna eggs, is a favorite all along the southwest coast of the island and is considered to be Sardinia's own caviar.

Some of the different types of dried pasta we see today could have originated from traditional Sardinian pasta, which was typically left to dry in the sunny open air. Some examples of these are *fregula*, which is a pasta prepared by rolling durum wheat flour and water into tiny balls and toasting it. In Cagliari this is served with clams. *Culurgiones* are *ravioli* with a variety of fillings (*ricotta*, saffron, mint, meat, and prawns), and *malloreddus* are tiny little pasta shells typically served with a hearty sausage and tomato sauce.

But it is perhaps bread that best illustrates the quality of Sardinian flour and one of the island's age-old traditions. Each region boasts its own specialty bread, made with special techniques and according to ancient recipes. Of these, one of the most famous is *pane carasau*, wafer-thin sheets of toasted bread also known as *carta da musica* (sheet music). This bread is typical of the Barbagia region and was a staple part of the shepherds' diets, together with *pane frattau*, a sort of pie made from *pane carasau*, baked with tomato sauce, *pecorino*, and boiled eggs.

Finally, we need a well-deserved mention for the island's desserts. *Sebadas* are round, sweet *ravioli* filled with cheese, which are fried and covered in honey. The specialty biscuits of Ozieri are the *sospiri*, while Tonara is famous for Sardinian *nougat*. The Campidano region offers delicious *gueffus* and *candelau*, the Barbagia has its *piricchittus* and *pabassinas*, while throughout the island there are numerous delicious and elegant biscuits made from almonds and sweet cheeses.

Right: Sunset on the Sardinian coast

Anguilla nella foglia di vite

Eel wrapped in vine leaves

serves 8

4 slices of white bread, crusts removed and cubed

2 tbsp butter, melted

8 sage leaves, finely chopped

2 tbsp fresh thyme

1 large garlic clove, finely chopped

juice of 1 lemon

4 tbsp dry white wine or sherry

salt and black pepper

1 eel, weighing at least 2 lbs, washed, gutted, skinned, and cut into 1½-inch chunks

16 vine leaves, washed and dried

olive oil, for brushing

This is a very traditional *canapé* or *antipasto* from the island's capital city of Cagliari. If eel proves hard to find or is just too strong in flavor for your taste, then monkfish or hake will also work very well. If fresh vine leaves are also hard to find, you could use bottled vine leaves instead (for making *dolmades*—available at all good Turkish or Greek food stores) or the strong, dark green outer leaves of a cos or romaine lettuce.

Fry the bread gently in the butter until golden brown and crisp, then add the herbs and garlic and mix together.

Add the lemon juice and the wine and mix together over the heat, for a minute or two or until the alcohol has all evaporated, then season and set aside.

Spread out the vine leaves and place a chunk of eel in the center of each one. Cover with a teaspoon of the bread mixture and wrap the leaf closed. Brush with olive oil, secure with cook's string or a toothpick, and place on the barbecue, chargrill pan, or under a hot grill for about three minutes on each side before serving.

Crostini di bottarga

Sardinian dried fish roe on toast

serves 8

10 oz tuna roe

16 small squares of toasted bread

juice of 1 lemon

3 tbsp chopped flat-leaf parsley

4 tbsp extra virgin olive oil

black pepper

Bottarga is the salted, cured roe of fish such as gray or red mullet or tuna. Hugely prized as a main ingredient in Sardinian cuisine, it is a valuable source of protein and was thus much appreciated by sailors and fishermen on long voyages. It is used in pasta dishes, *risotto*, salads, and served simply on warm toast as a *canapé* or *antipasto*. Please note that the flavor of the *bottarga* varies according to the fish that it comes from. This recipe calls for tuna *bottarga*, but you may prefer one of the other varieties.

Slice the tuna roe very carefully and thinly with a mandolin.

Arrange on top of the toast. Sprinkle with the lemon juice, parsley, olive oil, and black pepper and serve.

Right: Crostini di bottarga

Carpaccio di spada e rucola

Carpaccio of swordfish and arugula

serves 4

8 thin slices ciabatta
or casareccio bread,
lightly toasted on
both sides

6 tbsp extra virgin
olive oil

10 oz very fresh, raw
swordfish
(thoroughly chilled
to aid slicing)

juice of 1 lemon

salt and white pepper

large handful of
arugula

Although the original recipe for *carpaccio* is from Venice (named after the famous fifteenth-century painter of the same name in memory of his expert use of veal-hued pink paint) the word *carpaccio* has since gone on to mean any dish that uses raw ingredients that are sliced paper-thin, to the point of translucency. This recipe for swordfish is from the town of Cagliari.

Arrange the toasted bread on a serving dish. Drizzle with half the oil.

Slice the swordfish with a mandolin into paper-thin slices and drape these on top of the toasted bread.

Drizzle with the lemon juice and season with the salt and pepper.

Scatter the arugula on top, drizzle with the remaining oil, and serve at once.

Bocconcini di tonno con pancetta e olive

Tuna bites with olives and pancetta

serves 8

large handful of green
olives, pitted and
chopped

salt and black pepper

14 oz fresh tuna, cubed

7 oz smoked pancetta,
thinly sliced

1½ tbsp butter

4–5 sage leaves, very
finely chopped

This delightful recipe, full of flavor and great textures, comes from the Sardinian town of Oristano.

Mix the chopped olives with salt and pepper and mix with the cubed tuna. Preheat the oven to 400°F.

Wrap each cube of tuna, coated in the chopped olives, in a slice of smoked *pancetta* and secure with a wooden toothpick.

Lightly butter an ovenproof dish and lay the *bocconcini* in the dish. Sprinkle with the chopped sage and bake for about 10 minutes, turning them all over halfway through. Remove from the oven and serve at once.

Right: Carpaccio di spada e rucola

Impanadas di pesce

Fish empanadas

serves 8

1¾ cups semolina

4 oz butter, cubed

salt and black pepper

1 lb fish fillets (bass,
    bream, dentex, or
    similar)

8 tbsp extra virgin
    olive oil

1 large onion, chopped

2 tbsp chopped
    flat-leaf parsley

¼ tsp grated nutmeg

1 tsp saffron powder
    (preferably Sardinian)

flour, for dusting

1 egg, beaten

butter, for greasing

These traditional little Sardinian pies come from the town of Sassari. Originally made using the highly prized fish called a *dentice* (dentex), it can be made with any kind of flavorsome white fish, such as sea bass or bream.

Make a pastry dough with the *semolina*, butter, a pinch of salt, and enough cold water to just pull everything together into a soft ball of dough. Put it somewhere warm to rest for about 30 minutes, wrapped in plastic wrap or a clean cloth napkin.

Carefully check the fish fillets for bones, then fry gently in the olive oil until cooked through. Remove the fish from the oil and set aside. Add the onion to the same pan and fry in the remaining oil until softened.

Add the parlsey, nutmeg, saffron powder, and some salt and pepper to the pan and stir into the onion, then return the fish to the pan and mix together, breaking up the fillets.

Preheat the oven to 375°F. Roll out the pastry dough thinly on a lightly floured surface and, using a cookie cutter or an upturned glass, cut about 40 circles with a one-and-a-half-inch diameter. Put a spoonful of the fish mixture into the center of half the circles.

Cover with all the remaining circles and press around the edges with the tines of a fork to seal them all closed. Brush with beaten egg and lay on a buttered baking tray.

Bake for about 20 minutes, or until crisp and golden, then serve at once.

Frittatina di ricotta

Mini ricotta frittata

serves 4

1 large onion, finely chopped

1 green chilli pepper, de-seeded and finely chopped

1 stick unsalted butter

2 tbsp plain white flour

7 fl oz cold milk

salt and black pepper

7 oz hard grating ricotta (or more of the pecorino)

4 oz strong grating pecorino (the stronger the better)

4 eggs, beaten

This is a recipe from the Sardinian town of Nuoro. If the hard grating *ricotta* proves hard to obtain, just use the same quantity of stronger *pecorino* instead.

In a large frying pan, fry the onion and chilli together gently in about half the butter until softened.

Sift the flour over the onion and chilli and mix together over a low heat to incorporate without lumps forming, then add all the milk and mix together until thickened. Season with salt and pepper and leave to cool.

Mix the cheeses with the beaten eggs in a bowl and season with salt and pepper. Then mix in the cooled onion and chilli mixture.

Melt the butter in a small frying pan and pour in the mixture to make several little *frittata*, letting it cook on one side by tipping the pan and moving the mixture around, keeping it all reasonably flat, then tip the *frittata* over on to a plate and sliding it back into the pan the other way up to cook on the other side until golden.

Slide the cooked *frittata* out on to a board, cool slightly then cut into cubes or wedges and serve just warm.

TUSCANY

While the landscape of Tuscany is quite varied, from the ancient marble quarries of the Apuan Alps to the sand dunes of the Tyrrhenian Coast, it is the land between, in particular the Chianti district and the famous cities of Florence, Siena, Pisa, Arezzo, Volterra, and Lucca, that most readily come to mind when most people think about Tuscany. In this lovely region, hilltop towns and little villages dating back to Etruscan times are surrounded by neat vineyards where the vines form geometrically precise rows and olive groves alternate with rolling fields of wheat, corn, or sunflowers. The landscape explodes into a riot of color in the spring with the sudden arrival of the vibrant red poppies and the wild calendula with its little orange flowers. This is a landscape that has changed very little since the Middle Ages.

Tuscany's food is very much like Tuscany's landscape: soothingly simple; never too dramatic or challenging. Over time, Tuscan cooks have built up a repertoire of dishes with a clever interplay of their favorite ingredients, and they are masters of the art of understatement, which belies their natural sense of superiority.

According to my Tuscan relatives, it was the Tuscans who taught the French how to cook. According to popular Tuscan belief, French cuisine as we know it today was founded at the French court of Henry II, whose kitchen was staffed by Tuscan cooks imported by his Florentine wife, the 12-year-old Caterina de' Medici. Caterina's kitchens were responsible for introducing *pâté*; sweet and sour flavorings with meat, fish, and vegetables; ice cream; white sauce; and many other recipes and techniques to the French and their kitchens.

But the genius of Tuscan cooking actually lies in its simplicity. Fancy sauces aren't needed to hide the food because Tuscans use pure, strong flavors and the very freshest of seasonal ingredients. The great dishes are in fact very basic: homemade ribbons of egg pasta in a simple hare sauce, game or free-range domestic animal meats grilled over scented wood fire embers, and beans simmered in earthenware pots. The rest of Italy calls the Tuscans *I Mangiafagioli*, The Beaneaters, because they always seem to have a dish of beans on the table as an accompaniment to their main dish or as part of the *antipasto*, soup, pasta sauce, or casserole.

Tuscans make generous use of their seasonings, especially salt, pepper, and fresh herbs such as rosemary. One of the most prominent cooking additions is a splash of the local wine, and the superb local olive oil is used as both a cooking fat and a dressing. The use of butter is rare, and the traditional bread is made without the addition of salt.

Tuscan olive oil is some of the finest in the entire world, especially oil produced around the city of Lucca, and comes in several different versions depending on where the trees have been grown, but always uses the same variety of olive to give the oil its unmistakable peppery quality.

Right: Orcia Valley, Tuscany

Crostini Toscani

Tuscan pâté on toast

serves 4

½ an onion, finely chopped

1 carrot, finely chopped

1 celery stick, finely chopped

3 tbsp olive oil

1 tbsp butter

1 chicken liver, trimmed and washed

4 oz calves' liver, trimmed, washed, and dried

2 tbsp dry white wine

1 heaped tbsp tomato paste, diluted in 4 tbsp hot water

salt and black pepper

1 oz capers, rinsed and finely chopped

4 or 8 thin slices crusty white or brown bread

1 tbsp finely chopped flat-leaf parsley

Some say that this is the original, fifteenth-century recipe for *pâté* from the Medici kitchens, and that it was then exported to France along with other recipes, such as onion soup and ice cream. Whatever its provenance, it is a delicious way to sharpen the appetite at the start of a meal. In Tuscany, the word *crostini* traditionally refers to this *pâté*, as opposed to "toasted bread with various toppings" that it has since come to mean.

Fry the vegetables in the olive oil and half of the butter. Cook until soft and then add the liver.

Add the wine and stir for two minutes to evaporate the alcohol. Add the diluted tomato paste.

Season with salt and pepper, add two tablespoons of water, cover, and simmer for 20 minutes.

Remove the frying pan from the heat, lift the livers out of the sauce, and mince by hand or in the food processor until smooth. Return the semi-puréed livers to the pan.

Stir in the rest of the butter and the capers. Heat through, then remove from the heat and keep warm.

Spread the bread generously with the *pâté*, sprinkle with parsley, and serve.

Hints and tips:

Salted capers are generally considered to have a better flavor than those that are pickled in vinegar or preserved in brine. However, do be mindful of the salt content and rinse the capers thoroughly several times before use. It is a good idea to taste one to see if you have rinsed enough before adding them to the dish.

Torta di nasello

Savory hake cake

serves 6–8

2 cups dry white wine

1 onion, thinly sliced

8 small fillets of hake

1 lb 4 oz wild
mushrooms

1 tbsp olive oil

1 tbsp chopped
flat-leaf parsley

salt and black pepper

8 tbsp prepared
béchamel sauce
(see page 60)

4 oz pecorino, grated

6 tbsp heavy cream

8 oz all-butter
short-crust pastry

butter, for greasing

The flavors of the field and the sea combine with wonderful results in this Tuscan recipe. Perfect for a summer lunch.

Pour two cups of cold water into a pan and add the wine and onion. Bring to a boil, then add the fish, and simmer gently until cooked. Remove the fish from the pan, and cool before flaking roughly. Strain the remaining liquid and return it to the pan. Cook over a medium heat to reduce the stock to one third.

Clean and slice all the mushrooms and place them in a pan with the oil and parsley to cook until soft. Season and leave to cool.

In a large bowl, mix together the *béchamel*, mushrooms, and *pecorino*. Season and stir in the cream and the reserved liquid. Preheat the oven to 375°F.

Roll out the pastry on a floured surface and use it to line a well-greased pie pan. Blind bake the pastry as directed on the packet, then remove it from the oven and cool slightly. Fill the pastry with a layer of the *béchamel* and mushroom mixture. Cover this with the fish, then cover with more of the mushroom mixture and bake for a further five to 10 minutes, or until firm. Remove from the oven and cool slightly before serving.

Seppioline ripiene

Stuffed baby squid

serves 8

1 garlic clove, crushed

4 tbsp olive oil

9 large tomatoes,
peeled, deseeded,
and chopped

salt and black pepper

2 lbs small squid,
cleaned

1 egg, beaten

¼ cup fresh bread
crumbs

¼ cup parmesan,
grated

grated zest of ½
lemon

2 tbsp chopped
flat-leaf parsley

Here is another recipe that calls for sun-ripened tomato and garlic paired with *parmesan* and fruits of the sea.

Fry the garlic in the olive oil for about five minutes. Add the tomatoes and season to taste. Simmer this sauce for about 30 minutes, adding a little water occasionally and stirring frequently. You need to end up with enough sauce to lightly cover the squid.

Wash and dry the squid, then remove the tentacles to leave just the tubular body for stuffing. Chop the tentacles finely and set aside.

Mix the egg with the bread crumbs, tentacles, *parmesan*, lemon zest, and flat-leaf parsley. Season to taste and then spoon even quantities into each squid. Do not overfill, as this mixture will swell a bit during cooking.

Sew the squid closed carefully with cook's string using a tapestry needle, or close them with a wooden toothpick.

Lower them into the sauce, cover, and simmer very gently for about an hour, or until tender. Serve hot or cold, removing the string if used.

Arancini di Farro al tonno

Farro arancini with tuna

serves 8

1 onion, chopped

4 oz butter

7 oz farro (or spelt)

2 cups chicken or
vegetable stock

4 oz parmesan, grated

14 oz canned tuna,
drained

4 egg yolks

salt and black pepper

2 eggs, beaten with
2 tbsp water

5 tbsp dried bread
crumbs

8 thin slices of cheese
such as bel paese
or mild cheddar

4 cups sunflower oil
for deep-frying

This is another delicious way of using the traditional Tuscan grain called *farro*, a close relative of spelt, which is much-used in this region for salads and soups. Spelt will need soaking before use, whereas *farro* can be used immediately.

Fry the onion gently in half the butter until soft, then add the *farro* and toast it all over in the butter with onion. Add the stock and simmer, stirring until cooked through. Stir in the remaining butter and half the *parmesan* and leave to cool.

In a separate bowl, flake the tuna, mix with the egg yolks and the remaining *parmesan*, and season with salt and pepper. Mix in the *farro* mixture. Put the beaten eggs in a shallow bowl and spread the bread crumbs out on a tray.

Shape the tuna mixture into 16 small balls. Make a hollow in the center with your thumb and push half a slice of cheese into each one. Cover with more of the mixture, and then roll the little balls in the beaten egg, and then in the bread crumbs, taking care to shake off any excess.

Heat a wok or large, heavy-based pan containing the oil. When it starts to smoke, drop a crust of bread in. If the oil starts to froth around the bread and the bread turns golden, it is ready and you can start frying the *arancini* in batches until they are crisp and golden. Drain them thoroughly on paper towels to remove any excess oil before serving.

Fett'unta

Tuscan oil and garlic toast

makes 2 slices

2 thumb-thick slices of
good Tuscan bread

2 garlic cloves, peeled

plenty of very good
Tuscan olive oil

I think this is the ultimate garlic bread, made in the traditional Tuscan way. To be a real traditionalist, use unsalted Tuscan bread, but I have found it difficult to find outside a specific area around Florence and Siena. Use the best Tuscan olive oil in this recipe, one with plenty of peppery bite and a deep green flavor of freshly cut grass.

Toast the bread lightly until golden on both sides.

Rub the bread thoroughly with the garlic, then drench the bread with the oil so that it is slightly dripping and softened. This is wonderful served on its own, but also delicious with thinly sliced *prosciutto*, *salami*, or *mortadella*.

Ficattole con aglio e acciughe

Mini bread rolls with garlic and anchovies

serves 8

8 garlic cloves, peeled

1 heaped tbsp anchovy paste

6 tbsp fresh white bread crumbs soaked in 4 tbsp white wine vinegar and lightly squeezed dry

4 tbsp dry white wine

2 cups all-purpose flour, plus a little for dusting

3 tbsp fresh yeast

salt

4 cups sunflower oil for deep-frying

Another mouth-watering combination of flavors from the hills and the sea comes together in these rolls.

Pound the garlic in a mortar with a pestle until it is a smooth paste. Stir in the anchovy paste and the bread crumbs. Transfer this mixture to a small frying pan and add the wine. Bring to a boil and simmer gently for one or two minutes to evaporate the alcohol. Leave to cool.

Tip the flour onto the work surface. Put the yeast in a separate bowl or cup with five tablespoons of warm water and stir. Make a hollow in the center of the flour with your fist and pour in the dissolved yeast and a large pinch of salt. Knead together, adding more water as necessary, until you have a smooth, pliable ball of dough.

Put the dough in an oiled bowl, cover, and leave to rise in a warm spot for about one hour. Remove the dough from the bowl, knock back, and then roll out on a lightly floured surface to a quarter-inch thickness. Cut into long, thick strips with a pastry wheel.

Heat a wok or large, heavy-based pan containing the oil. When it starts to smoke, drop a crust of bread in. If the oil starts to froth around the bread and the bread turns golden, it is ready and you can start frying the *ficattole* in batches for three to four minutes, until crisp and golden. Drain the *ficattole* on paper towels. Arrange on a dish to serve, and sprinkle with the garlic sauce.

UMBRIA

Umbria's food is always very hearty, with plenty of game, cured pork, spelt, lentils, and (of course) the ubiquitous black truffle. Interestingly, some historians consider this style of cooking and eating to be very similar to that of the Etruscans, who occupied much of the region before 300 BC. Olives, anchovies, artichokes, and capers have all become primary ingredients in the local cuisine, paired with pork, wood pigeon, and wild game, especially boar.

In this region, ancient spit-roasting techniques are still very popular and used to great effect. Game is turned slowly on a spit while being brushed with *la ghiotta*, the medieval marinade made with red wine, olive oil, chopped pancetta, capers, vinegar, olives, anchovies, onion, garlic, cloves or juniper berries, sage, and lemon juice. They say it is a recipe that has remained unchanged for hundreds of years.

Umbrian food can best be defined by the use of very few, largely wild, ingredients. It is rich in flavor but cooked simply. The most obvious example (and also coincidentally the most prized ingredient of this entire region) is the truffle, *il tartufo*. The season for truffles begins in the fall and lasts throughout the winter. They are expertly sniffed out from under the soil by specially trained dogs. Truffles are a highly valued treasure from the rich earth; the places where they grow are closely guarded secret passed on from one generation to the next. The most highly prized truffles are those found in the Spoleto and Norcia areas. Black truffles generally come from Valnerina while white truffles are harvested from the Upper Tevere Valley. The truffle is so highly coveted in Umbria that in the fall and winter there are numerous festivals and markets all over the region to celebrate these precious nuggets.

The small town of Norcia should also be noted for its famous skill in the butchering and curing of pork, and the production of *salumi*. There is even a word used to define this special skill: *norcineria*.

Antipasti in Umbria also reflect this region's best produce and their philosophy of using very few ingredients with carefully honed skill. It can be as simple as a variety of perfectly toasted *bruschetta* topped with olive or truffle pastes, a platter of grilled vegetables dressed with the region's exceptional olive oil, or a selection of the region's exceptional *salumi* from Norcia. The simple *frittata* is another popular starter, flavored with cheese, sautéed greens, fresh herbs, or leftover vegetables. In the spring, fava beans dressed with olive oil and *pecorino* cheese are often served, while in the fall, when olive oil is harvested, *antipasti* may include *pinzimonio*, fresh vegetables dipped in seasoned olive oil, or *fett'unta*, toasted bread drizzled with the new olive oil and sprinkled with sea salt.

Among the desserts of note, which are usually only served for very special occasions, there are *torciglione*, a serpent-shaped sweet made of ground almonds, flour, and sugar; *baci di San Francesco* (kisses of Saint Francis); *biscottini delle monache* (little nun's biscuits); and *ciaramicola*, (the sweetheart cake), which is a pink cake flavored with Alchermes liqueur and topped with icing and colored sprinkles. This cake is associated with both Easter and with love, and it is traditional for a young woman to bake this cake for her sweetheart. The *rocciata di Assisi* is a spiral shaped pastry very similar to strudel, made in slightly different versions in both Foligno and Spoleto. *Frittelle di San Giuseppe* is typical of Orvieto and deep-fried for the city's patron saint on his feast day, March 19. Other Umbrian sweets include *brustengolo* (*polenta* cake), *maccheroni dolci* (sweet pasta), *pinoccate* (pine nut biscuits), and *panpepato* (a peppery, spiced, fruit cake) popular at Christmas.

Right: The view from Torre del Moro towards the town of Orvieto, Umbria

Arvoltori di Perugia

Pancetta and rosemary pancakes

serves 4

4 tbsp all-purpose
  flour
sea salt
4 oz thickly cut
  pancetta or streaky
  bacon, cubed
1 sprig of rosemary
8 tbsp extra virgin
  olive oil

This is a very traditional recipe from the city of Perugia, the regional capital of Umbria.

In a large mixing bowl, make a batter with the flour, a pinch of salt, and enough water as required to create a texture like custard.

Add the cubes of pancetta or bacon.

Strip all the leaves off the rosemary and chop them finely. Stir these into the batter.

Heat some of the oil in a wide, shallow, nonstick pan, and cook the batter like you would do for pancakes, flipping them after about three minutes. Cook on the other side for a further two minutes.

Roll them up and sprinkle with salt before cutting into triangles and serving piping hot.

Torcoletti di Todi

Baked cheese twists

serves 10

1¾ lbs yeast bread
  dough
2 eggs, beaten
3–4 tbsp extra
  virgin olive oil
4 oz pecorino, grated
4 oz parmesan, grated
salt
oil, for greasing

This recipe originated in the lovely town of Todi.

Knead the bread dough with the eggs and the oil, then add the cheeses and knead them into the dough too. Let the resulting dough rise, covered with a cloth, in a warm place for about one hour or until doubled in volume.

Grease a baking tray, or several trays, thoroughly and preheat the oven to 400°F.

Punch down the dough and roll it out into a long cylinder about the thickness of your thumb. Cut into sections about two inches long and twist these into a loop, almost like the start of a knot.

Lay these on the oiled baking trays and bake for about 20 minutes, or until crisp and golden.

Serve hot or at room temperature.

Right: Arvoltori di Perugia

Fiori di zucchine ripieni alla Ternana

Stuffed zucchini flowers

makes 20

20 zucchini flowers

3 cups leftover risotto

2 eggs

salt and black pepper

1 cup all-purpose flour

3½ oz parmesan, grated

sunflower oil, for frying

This delicious recipe for zucchini blossoms comes from the Umbrian town of Terni.

Wash the blossoms carefully, leaving the squash or courgette attached if possible, and lay them out on paper towels until dry. Place a tablespoon of leftover *risotto* into each flower, and gently twist the flowers at the top.

Crack the eggs into a bowl, season with salt and pepper, then whisk thoroughly. Add the flour and whisk again. When the batter is smooth, whisk in the *parmesan* and dip the flowers in carefully. Heat the oil until sizzling, and then drop the blossoms into the hot oil. Fry until crisp and golden, then scoop the fritters out of the oil and drain on paper towels to remove excess oil. Sprinkle with salt and serve at once.

Pecorino e fave

Pecorino with fresh fava beans

serves 4 to 6

2 lbs fresh fava
beans, podded and
peeled if necessary

11 oz pecorino

When fava beans first come into season in Umbria and also in other parts of Italy, they are considered best enjoyed with chunks of *pecorino* and some good red wine. It is preferable to use beans that are young enough not to need peeling, but if they do need peeling, a quick blanch in boiling water makes the job a lot easier!

Prepare the beans first and arrange on a plate.

Shave the *pecorino* and scatter over the beans, or serve it in little chunks.

When serving, encourage your guests to eat the beans and the cheese together.

EMILIA ROMAGNA

The big, rich, fertile region of Emilia Romagna is known as the gastronomic heartland of Italy, producing up to 60 percent of all the produce eaten in Italy. This intensely passionate and food-loving region, with the ancient city of Bologna as its capital (known as *Bologna la grassa*, Bologna the fat one!) is famous for being the place where fresh pasta was first created. It is also the home of traditional balsamic vinegar, *prosciutto di Parma,* and *parmigiano reggiano*, among many other well known staples of Italian cuisine. Throughout the entire region, each and every town and village has its own culinary specialties that are truly remarkable and unique.

Bordering six other regions, this extremely fertile land skirts both the Po River and the Apennines. Most of the region's most important towns lie on the Via Emilia, a road built in Roman times that cuts a path from Piacenza at the top of the region to Rimini on the Adriatic Sea. The area from Bologna to the north is Emilia; from Bologna to the south is Romagna. Bologna is located in the center and draws many characteristics from both Emilia and Romagna.

The foods of both halves of this region are robust, full of flavor, and absolutely distinctive.

In Emilia Romagna, *tagliatelle, lasagne,* and *tortellini* are favorites, and their preparation cannot be rivaled anywhere else in the country. *La sfoglia* is an integral part of the local menu, more important than bread or olive oil.

The local figure of the housewife, known as the *azdora* in the local dialect, is the central, solid hub around which the entire family revolves. This very traditional and matriarchal culture ensures that in this region, the *azdora* remains queen of the household.

In Parma they say, "The pig is like the music of Verdi. It's all good; there's nothing to throw away." Pork is one of the most important cornerstones of Emilia Romagna's cuisine. *Prosciutto crudo*, the most famous of Italy's pork products, is cured in the Langhirano Valley near Parma, where a favorable microclimate and the age-old tradition of salting and air-drying the ham ensures the best possible results. By strict law, the Parma ham pigs must be fed on the whey resulting from the production of *parmigiano reggiano*, which is said to make them fatter and sweeter, and creates an ongoing, unbroken exchange between these two very typical and traditional local products. *Parmigiano reggiano*, with each wheel made from 170 gallons of milk, has been made in the province of Parma for over 700 years.

Other cured meats, such as *coppa* and *pancetta*, are specialties of the town of Piacenza, farther north but not far from Parma. Only the most delicate meat and careful of seasoning techniques goes into making the famed *mortadella* of Bologna.

Farther south, Romagna is the land of the homemade *salami*, but this part of the region also has a strong tradition of fish dishes, including the tasty fish soups made from the fresh catch of the Adriatic—the delicious *brodetto*.

Another of Emilia Romagna's great culinary contributions is balsamic vinegar, which has been made in Modena for centuries and is still produced in the time-honored traditional methods regulated by the state.

Right: Greengrocer on Via Calzolerie, Bologna, Emilia-Romagna

Parmigiano al balsamico

Parmesan chunks with balsamic vinegar

makes 1 small
tray

3½ oz parmesan

balsamic vinegar

This is one of the simplest and most delicious ways to enjoy two of the most famous products of this region together. The key is to use the freshest, most crumbly and perfect *parmesan* and really good-quality, sweet, thick balsamic.

Cut the *parmesan* into small chunks and arrange them on a plate in a circle.

Pour the balsamic vinegar into a small bowl. Encourage your guests to dip the chunks of *parmesan* into the vinegar before eating. Offer toothpicks or small forks if you wish.

Mortadella, asparagi e parmigiano

Mortadella, asparagus, and parmesan

serves 4–6

11 oz small asparagus
   spears, cut in half
   lengthwise

7 oz mortadella, sliced
   and cut into long
   sticks

4 oz shaved parmesan

juice of ½ a lemon

1 heaped tbsp
   chopped fresh mint

4 tbsp chopped
   flat-leaf parsley

4 tbsp extra virgin
   olive oil

salt and black pepper

I like the simple, gentle flavor of *mortadella*—it makes a great base for other flavors.

For an elegant occasion, you can arrange the asparagus in one layer on a pretty plate, then cover with a layer of *mortadella*, sprinkle on the dressing, and finish off with the *parmesan* shavings.

Alternatively, put the asparagus, the *mortadella*, and the *parmesan* into a shallow bowl and mix them all up together, or wrap the dressed asparagus and *parmesan* in small cones made out of the *mortadella* slices.

To make the dressing, mix the lemon juice with the mint and parsley and add salt and pepper to taste. Add the oil and whisk thoroughly until the dressing thickens. Pour the dressing over the asparagus. Mix thoroughly and serve.

Left: Parmigiano al balsamico

Ravioli fritti

Deep-fried ravioli

serves 6

The dough:

7½ cups all-purpose flour, plus extra for dusting

4 tbsp extra virgin olive oil

2 tsp dried yeast

salt

2 tbsp extra virgin olive oil

salt and black pepper

4¼ cups sunflower oil for deep-frying

parmesan, grated, to serve

The filling:

1 lb ground beef

1 onion, finely chopped

Making *ravioli* by hand is a truly different cooking experience and the results are utterly delicious.

Make the dough by mixing together the flour, oil, yeast, and salt, adding just enough cold water to make a firm, pliable dough. It must not be in any way sticky, but should feel elastic and springy when gently pressed with a fingertip. Leave to rise for one hour, covered.

Fry the beef, onion, and oil together in a separate pan until the beef is well browned. Season with salt and pepper and leave to simmer gently for about 30 minutes, adding a little water if the mixture looks too dry. Remove from the heat and cool completely.

Roll out the dough as thinly as possible on a floured surface and cut it into circles about one-and-a-half-inches in diameter. Put a teaspoon of the cooled filling in the center of each circle, then fold in half and press closed with the tines of a fork to seal.

Heat a wok or large, heavy-based pan containing the oil. When it starts to smoke, drop a crust of bread in. If the oil starts to froth around the bread and the bread turns golden, it is ready and you can start frying the *ravioli* in batches, for about four minutes. Drain on paper towels and serve hot, sprinkled with a little *parmesan*.

Datteri al prosciutto

Dates wrapped in Parma ham

makes 20 canapés

1 tsp vegetable oil for greasing

20 dried dates

20 small cubes of parmesan or other hard cheese

10 slices of Parma ham, halved

The combination of the sweet flavor of the dates and the salty sweetness of the ham makes these little bites utterly delicious.

Preheat the oven to 375°F. Lightly grease a baking tray large enough to fit all the dates.

Remove the stone from the dates and replace the stone with a little cube of cheese.

Wrap each date in half a slice of Parma ham and fix each one closed with a wooden toothpick. Lay them on the lightly greased baking trays.

Bake for about 10 minutes, or until the ham starts to crisp up. Serve hot.

Right: Datteri al prosciutto

Biscotti al parmigiano

Parmesan biscuits

makes 24 biscuits

7 oz all-purpose flour

4 oz parmesan, grated

½ tsp dried thyme

1 tsp salt

½ garlic clove, chopped

large pinch of cayenne pepper

5 tbsp unsalted butter

These are the most delicious biscuits imaginable – truly irresistible!

Preheat the oven to 375°F. Line several baking sheets with nonstick parchment paper.

Mix the flour with three ounces of the *parmesan*, thyme, salt, garlic, and cayenne pepper, using a food processor if you wish. Rub in the butter if making it by hand, or use the food processor on pulse to incorporate it into the dry ingredients to make a smooth ball of pastry. Take care not to work the dough too much or it will become brittle and heavy.

Divide the dough in half and roll each half out like a sausage, on a floured surface, to a length of about 12 inches. Using a sharp knife, cut into one-inch rounds.

Lay the cut biscuits on the lined baking trays, allowing about two inches of space between each. Squash the rounds down slightly with your fingertips to make them about two inches across. Sprinkle with the remaining *parmesan*.

Bake for about 15 minutes, or until crisp and golden brown. Once baked, remove from the baking trays and cool on wire racks before serving. They will also keep very well for several days in an airtight container.

Costolettine d'agnello alla Bolognese

Mini lamb cutlets in the Bolognese style

serves 6

12 tiny lamb cutlets

3 tbsp all-purpose flour

2 eggs, beaten

5 tbsp dried white bread crumbs

6 tbsp olive oil (not extra virgin)

salt and black pepper

5 oz mozzarella, cut into 12 slices

4 oz prosciutto crudo, in very thin slices

A marvelous recipe for tender spring lamb cutlets from Emilia Romagna. For this to be a *canapé*, you will need to seek out the smallest and tenderest lamb cutlets you can find.

Preheat the oven to 425°F.

Trim the cutlets carefully and flatten them as much as possible with a meat mallet. Dip them lightly in the flour, then dip them in egg, and finally in the bread crumbs. Heat the oil until sizzling, then fry the lamb cutlets on each side until golden brown and crisp.

Remove from the pan, drain thoroughly on paper towels, and season to taste.

Arrange the cutlets on a baking tray. Lay a slice of *mozzarella* on each cutlet and wrap in a slice of ham. Then bake in the oven for five to six minutes, or until the cheese begins to melt. Transfer to a serving platter and serve at once.

Left: Biscotti al parmigiano

Overleaf: Piazza Grande, Modena

LIGURIA

Ligurian cuisine is largely distinguished from other regional Italian cuisines because Liguria is the only Italian region that borders with the sea to the south, the Alps to the north, and the Apennines to the east. It benefits from the temperate climate of the Tyrrhenian Sea and draws protection from the natural barrier of the mountains which preventing the passage of icy winds from the north. This climate, together with the historic and commercial tradition of the port of Genova, has created a unique gastronomy, combining the traditions of food prepared to suit the needs and desires for returning sailors starved of fresh food after months at sea with the best that the region has to offer.

The food of Liguria is in many ways representative of the area's unique climate, using many ingredients, such as lemons and oranges, that would not normally be considered to be northern ingredients but which flourish in this most beautiful region, nicknamed the Italian Riviera. In a region where there is little or no flat land for growing large quantities of crops, scented herbs can be grown in any sunny corner or on a windowsill.

The most famous of all culinary masterpieces from Liguria is its basil *pesto* sauce, served with either *trofie* as favored in the Cinque Terre, or with *trenette* as favored in Genova, where it often also combined with boiled potatoes and green beans, as well as with pasta itself.

Wheat, chickpeas, and chestnuts from the hills and mountains are all used to make flour for bread and pasta. The olive oil of the region is one of the lightest and most floral of the entire country, perfect with the region's staple diet of vegetables, fish, and pasta. It is known as *Riviera Ligure* and is protected by a PDO designation.

Seafood plays a large role in the local diet, especially the much-loved silvery anchovies, which are a favorite *antipasto*, as part of a fish soup, or as a main course. Sardines, emperor bream, gray and red mullet, gurnard, and sea bass are also popular, as well as mussels and razor clams.

Rabbit and veal appear often on the menu as popular, traditional meat dishes such as *tomaxelle* (stuffed veal rolls) or *coniglio con le olive*, (casserole of rabbit with olives).

But it really is green vegetables that take pride of place in Liguria, crammed into pies with a paper-thin pastry casing to make *torta verde* (green cake) or gently baked in the oven with a delicious filling and smothered in fabulous Ligurian olive oil.

The rocky coastline of Liguria and its soaring hills and mountains does not provide much room for dairy cows (and therefore cheese production), but imports from other regions of Italy have been used in many of the local dishes, most notably the use of *parmigiano reggiano* for adding to *pesto*, and *stracchino* or *crescenza* to make the famous *focaccia al formaggio* from the town of Recco. *Pecorino* and also *ricotta* are also often used.

Ligurian desserts include *pandolce Genovese*, a sweet bread made with candied fruit, raisins, and nuts, and a sweet *"pizza"* made with walnuts, chestnuts, and candied fruit. The mountains and hills are also rich in wild berries, such as raspberries, tiny strawberries, and deep purple myrtleberries, all of which are used in open-face tarts and jam.

Right: The view towards the village of Manarola on the Ligurian Riviera

Focaccia al formaggio

Focaccia with cheese

serves 6

2¼ lbs all-purpose
flour

½ cup extra virgin
olive oil

salt

2 cups water

4¼ lbs crescenza or
stracchino

2–3 tbsp olive oil, for
greasing and
drizzling

The famous *focaccia di recco* is a deliciously cheesy variation of
the other types of *focaccia* you'll find all over Liguria. This one is
made by stretching out a thin sheet of dough, dotting it generously
with a creamy, sour curd cheese called *crescenza* (or *stracchino*),
covering with another sheet of dough, then baking. The result is
wonderful, and there was a time not so long ago when the people of
Genova used to take day-trips to Recco just to enjoy this specialty.

If you can't get hold of either *crescenza*, *stracchino*, or a similar
cheese such as *prescinseua*, you will need to find a cheese that is
mild and creamy enough to be spreadable, not too liquid, and will
melt when cooked.

Tip the flour into a mound on a clean surface. Make a well in the center with
your fist, then pour in the olive oil, salt, and about half a cup of water. Knead
everything together, adding enough water to eventually achieve a soft, smooth
dough. Knead it well for 15 minutes, then cover it with a cloth and let it rest in
an oiled bowl for half an hour at room temperature.

After it has rested, divide the dough into an equal number of pieces (two per
focaccia, and the size of the *focacce* will be dictated by the size of your baking pans
and your oven). If you are making lots of little *focaccine*, you will need to make
the balls very small.

Don't roll the dough out; use your fingers instead to stretch it into a sheet,
working with your hands as it thins out, until it is really very thin—less than
one-sixteenth of an inch. Be careful not to puncture the dough as you work it.

Lay half the sheets of dough on an oiled baking tray and dot with cheese.
Lay the second sheets of dough over the first, and curl the edges in, squeezing
them tightly to make a seal.

Press the top sheet down around the cheese balls, and pierce the dough in
a number of places to allow steam to escape as it cooks.

Sprinkle the *focaccia* with any remaining olive oil and sprinkle with salt.

Heat the oven to 475°F, or as hot as your oven will go.

Bake the *focaccias* in batches for about four minutes, or until golden brown
with darker bubbles and variations in color. Slide out onto a board, slice, and
serve immediately while the bread is oozing cheese.

Hints and tips:

You will need to get your oven exceptionally hot for this recipe.

Zucchine arrotolate al pesto e ricotta

Zucchini rolls with pesto and ricotta

makes 24

3 long but not too plump zucchini

6 tbsp ricotta

2 tbsp parmesan, grated

2 tsp pesto

2 tsp finely chopped flat-leaf parsley

salt and black pepper

24 chives

This recipe is a little bit particular, but the end result is quite spectacular and it ends up being rather sophisticated and very easy to eat.

Using a T-bar potato peeler or a mandolin, finely slice the zucchini lengthwise into long strips and leave them in a colander, sprinkled with a little salt, to drain for about half an hour.

While the zucchini drain, mix the *ricotta* and *parmesan* together in a small bowl, stir in the *pesto* and the parsley, then season with salt and pepper.

Rinse and dry the zucchini strips and lay them on a chopping board. Drop about a teaspoon of filling on each one and roll them up around it. Tie each strip closed with a chive and then stand them upright on a serving dish. Serve at once, or chill until required.

Erbe fritte

Deep-fried herbs

serves 4–6

4 oz all-purpose flour

1 bottle very fizzy, very cold mineral water

2 cups extra virgin olive oil, preferably from Liguria

24 medium to large sage leaves, rinsed and dried

20 small sprigs flat-leaf parsley, washed and dried

sea salt

This is absolutely the most typical *stuzzichino*—a snack to serve with drinks—of Liguria. A bit tricky to get right, but rich with the fragrance of fresh Ligurian herbs. Locals will recommend you make this in the middle of summer when the herbs are at their very best.

Tip the flour into a bowl and, whisking constantly, gradually pour in enough sparkling water to make a smooth, lump-free batter with the texture of custard.

Heat the oil until sizzling hot.

Dip the herbs in the batter, drain off the excess and then drop each one into the oil. Fry all the herbs in this way, in batches, for just one to two minutes, or until golden brown. Remove with a slotted spoon, drain on paper towels, sprinkle with salt, and serve at once.

Torta pasqualina

Easter pie

serves 8

2¾ cups all-purpose flour, plus extra for dusting

½ cup warm water

4 tbsp extra-virgin olive oil

1 large onion, chopped

6 artichokes preserved in oil

14 oz. fresh spinach leaves, washed

large handful of fresh flat-leaf parsley, chopped

1 lb ricotta

2 oz parmesan, freshly grated

6 eggs

sea salt and black pepper

The custom of serving a savory cake or pie is common in various parts of Italy, especially in regions such as Liguria and Le Marche, as well as in parts of the south. This recipe is for the traditional Easter savory cake, served traditionally on Easter Monday, though it is good to eat any time, and cut into small pieces, will make a perfect *stuzzichini*.

To make the pastry, mix the flour and a pinch of salt in a bowl. Add the water and half the oil and mix to a smooth dough. Knead for five minutes on a floured surface until soft and stretchy. Cover with plastic wrap and set aside for 15 minutes.

To make the filling, heat the remaining oil in a large pan over medium heat. Fry the onion for eight minutes, stirring occasionally. Stir in the artichokes and toss for a few minutes. Pile spinach on top, cover the pan, and wilt over a gentle heat. Set aside to cool slightly.

Put the filling mixture in a food processor with the parsley, cheeses, and three eggs. Season well with salt and pepper then pulse and set aside.

Preheat the oven to 425°F. Roll out two-thirds of the pastry into a large circle on a floured surface to a large circle. Use to line base and sides of a deep, 11-inch, loose-bottomed cake pan. Spoon in the filling. Smooth, make two deep indents, and crack in two eggs. Roll out remaining pastry to a circle and lay on top. Twist edges to seal. Beat remaining egg, brush over pastry, and sprinkle with sea salt. Bake for 30–35 minutes until golden. Slice and serve.

Bocconcini con menta e peperoncino

Mini mozzarella balls with mint and chilli

serves 4

9 oz bocconcini
mozzarella

¼ tsp dried chili
flakes

1 tsp chopped fresh
mint

1 ½ tbsp extra virgin
olive oil

Mozzarella originated in the southern regions of Italy, but migrant workers drawn to the wealthy ports of Liguria may have introduced the delicious cheese. Liguria has traditionally had a very adaptable food culture, absorbing the best of its visitors' cuisines.

Drain the *bocconcini* and place in a bowl. Sprinkle with the chili and mint and drizzle with the oil. Toss to coat each ball well. Cover and leave to marinate in the refrigerator for at least one hour. Allow the cheese to return to room temperature before serving.

Frittatina alle erbe

Mini frittata with fresh herbs

serves 4

1 bulb fresh garlic,
chopped

1 large scallion,
chopped

small bunch of mint,
washed, dried, and
chopped

small handful of
lemon balm, rinsed,
dried, and chopped

small handful of fresh
flat-leaf parsley,
rinsed, dried, and
chopped

small handful of fresh
chervil, rinsed,
dried, and chopped

3 tbsp extra virgin
olive oil

3 tbsp cold water

8 eggs, beaten

salt and black pepper

All sorts of local herbs go into the mixture, such as wild garlic leaves, wild hops, borage, chicory, and much more. These are combined with whatever is available in the vegetable garden, such as pea shoots, fava bean shoots, broccoli, arugula flowers, or tiny new-season artichokes. There is no limit to the possible combinations, so please view the ingredients list purely as a guideline.

Gently fry the garlic, scallion, and all the herbs with the oil and the water until softened. Season the beaten eggs with the salt and pepper. Pour the eggs into the pan, and combine.

Cook slowly, pulling the edges of the *frittata* toward the center and tipping the pan to set the *frittata* on one side without burning it. Cover the *frittata* with a plate larger than the pan. Turn the *frittata* over in one smooth movement, so that it lands safely with the other side facing up on the lid or a plate. Slide the *frittata* back into the hot pan.

Shake the *frittata* into position, flatten with a spatula as required, and cook until golden brown on the bottom. Slide out the *frittata* onto a platter and serve hot or cold.

Right: Bocconcini con menta e peperoncino

LOMBARDY

This is one of Italy's largest regions. It lies in the north of the country and shares a border with Switzerland.

Stretching from the Alps to the lowlands of the Po Valley, it is home to a wide range of landscapes, including its breathtaking mountain chain and the valleys of Valchiavenna, Valtellina, and Camonica.

If you've ever been to Lombardy, you may have noticed the frequent appearance of the color yellow in the local food. It's a custom that dates back to medieval times when the Lombard nobility would coat their food with gold before serving it to guests. Gold was widely believed to be the very best remedy for illness and an ingredient that promised good health for the consumer. Food was also prepared with gold just for the sake of pure decadence. In time, as gold became more expensive and valuable, the wily Lombards looked for ways to create the same effect without the cost of using gold. The famous golden *risotto alla Milanese* is just one reminder of this tradition.

Risotto alla Milanese gets its golden color and its flavor from the precious spice saffron. Legend has it that the dish came about when a Milanese painter decided to gild the *risotto* served at the wedding banquet of his patrons' daughter with saffron in order to get himself noticed by her father. *Risotto alla Milanese* is traditionally served with *ossobuco* (braised veal shank steak), but not with *gremolata*, as often happens outside of Italy.

Generous use of butter is the main hallmark of Milanese and Lombard cooking, as is the general preference for rice or *polenta* over pasta. Being landlocked, Lombardy has few notable fish specialties, but the meat, most especially veal, is a central part of the local menu.

Made with raisins, candied citrus fruit, and sometimes with a creamy or chocolate filling, *panettone* is a fluffy *brioche*-like bread. It may be tall or short, covered with chocolate, or flavored with various liquors, but it's the most obvious edible symbol of the Christmas season in Italy.

With its domed shape, *panettone* has graced Christmas tables in Milan, where it is claimed to have been invented, since at least the fifteenth century. The traditional recipe calls for using nothing but flour, yeast, sugar, top-quality butter, fresh eggs, and golden raisins.

In Lombardy, cheese is considered very important. *Taleggio* is named for a valley in the province of Bergamo, but it is in fact produced throughout Lombardy. Production of this soft, creamy, cow's milk cheese can be dated as far back as a thousand years, and was traditionally ripened in underground caves. Today, it is matured in climate-controlled cellars. *Taleggio* has a mild, somewhat acidic flavor and a subtle aroma that makes it ideal as an ingredient for many traditional Lombard dishes. Because it melts easily, *taleggio* is excellent in omelettes and crêpes, or as the base for a creamy pasta sauce. Other famous cheeses of this area include *gorgonzola, mascarpone, stracchino, squaquerone, bitto, grana lodigiano,* and many others.

Also very traditional and popular in Lombardy is the rather odd but very beautiful *mostarda di Cremona*, from the inland port city of Cremona on the River Po. It consists of candied fruits, such as cherries, figs, and pears, preserved in a thick, clear mixture of sugar syrup and white mustard. The result is a tangy condiment that is always served with *bollito misto*, the region's great dish of mixed boiled meats and vegetables, or used as an ingredient in many savory dishes.

The mountainous area of Lombardy is called Valtellina and it is a land of ancient flavors. Among the traditional specialties found here are *pizzoccheri* (pasta made with buckwheat), *sciatt* (fried cheese), *polenta taragna* (made with buckwheat flour), *bresaola* (cured salted beef), and *bisciola* (a rustic cake containing walnuts, figs, and raisins).

Right: Looking through the arcade in Palazzo Comune, Cremona, Lombardy

Asparagi al gorgonzola

Asparagus with gorgonzola

makes approx 30

14 oz asparagus

8 oz gorgonzola dolce

½ cup extra virgin olive oil

1 cup dry white wine

strip of lemon zest

2 tsp white wine vinegar

salt and black pepper

The combination of *gorgonzola* and asparagus may seem unusual, but these are both traditional products of this region, and they actually do work well together. *Gorgonzola* can be bought in a sweet (*dolce*) version or in a piquant (*piccante*) version. It is the sweet version, with a milder flavor, that works for this recipe.

Steam the asparagus spears until just tender, about five minutes.

Separately, blend together the *gorgonzola*, oil, wine, lemon peel, and vinegar. Season to taste and pour into a dipping bowl.

Arrange the warm or cold asparagus spears on a serving platter with the dipping sauce, and serve.

Sciatt

Crispy balls with a melted cheese center

serves 6

1 cup buckwheat flour

1 cup all-purpose flour

3 tbsp grappa

1¼ cups cold water

6 oz bitto (or similar)

sunflower oil, for frying

This is a very traditional snack from the city of Bergamo and ideally needs to be made with a local cheese called *bitto* (see note below), although a good-quality semi-hard cow's milk cheese that has some added sharpness would work well.

Make a batter with the flours, *grappa*, and enough water to make a thick, textured batter. Whisk for about 20 minutes, then cover and leave to rest for two hours.

Cut the cheese into cubes and heat the oil until it is sizzling. Scoop up a spoonful of the batter with a tablespoon, drop a piece of cheese into it, and slide it into the hot oil.

Wait until the fritters turn golden brown and the cheese is melted, then remove with a slotted spoon. Drain them on paper towels and serve very hot.

Note: bitto is an Italian DOP (Protected Geographical Status) cheese produced around the valleys of Valtellina in Lombardy. It owes its name to the small river called the Bitto that flows through the Valtellina Valley in this cheese-producing area. It is the quality of the grass that the animals feed on that influences the taste of the final product, and *bitto* is produced only in the summer months when the cows feed in the alpine meadows on a rich combination of grasses and wild flowers. The cheese is made with this cow's milk, to which between 10 and 20 percent of milk from a local breed of goat is added.

Left: Asparagi al gorgonzola

Crostatine di zucca

Pumpkin tartlets

These are so wonderful; there is a marvelous combination of flavors in these little tarts (you could of course make one big tart if you prefer). If you like making pastry, feel free to make your own, otherwise buy a packet of all-butter short-crust pastry, just because it is quicker and easier!

makes 10 ×
2¹/₂-in tarts

1¹/₂ lbs raw pumpkin
   or butternut squash
   peeled, deseeded
   and cut into slices

salt and black pepper

2 tbsp olive oil

4 onions, finely sliced

6 tbsp unsalted butter,
   plus extra for
   greasing

1 oz dried *porcini*
   mushrooms, soaked
   in hot water for at
   least 20 minutes
   or until softened

1 packet of all-butter
   short-crust pastry

2 eggs, beaten

4 oz parmesan,
   grated

flour, for dusting

Preheat the oven to 350°F. Line a baking tray with nonstick parchment paper and lay the slices of pumpkin or squash on the parchment, season, and drizzle with the oil, and then bake the pumpkin until soft, for about 20 minutes.

Cook the onions gently until melting soft and golden in the butter, adding water if required. Drain and squeeze the mushrooms dry, chop them, and add to the onions and cook for a further 20 minutes, with a little of the liquid in which the mushrooms were soaking to keep them from drying out too much. Remove from the heat and leave to cool completely.

Butter and flour several small pastry cases for the tartlets. Roll out the pastry on a floured surface and cut out circles. Line the pastry cases with the pastry circles.

Stir the eggs and the *parmesan* into the cooled onion and mushroom mixture, season, and use this to cover the bottom of each pastry case, then cover with slices of baked pumpkin, and finally cover with another thin layer of the onion and mushroom mixture.

Use any leftover pastry to create a lattice pattern on top of each tart. Bake for about 15 minutes, or until the pastry is crisp and golden, and serve warm.

Antipasto di salame al burro e prezzemolo

Antipasto with salami, butter, and parsley

This simple snack is remarkably satisfying and so easy to make.

serves 8

- 1 packet of all-butter short-crust pastry
- flour, for dusting
- 2 garlic cloves, crushed
- 4 tbsp mayonnaise
- 6 tbsp salted butter, plus extra for greasing
- 4 tbsp finely chopped flat-leaf parsley
- salt and black pepper
- 4 oz salami Milano, cut into strips

Preheat the oven to 375°F. Roll out the pastry to a thickness of a quarter-inch and cut into circles the same size as your smallest tart pans. Butter and flour the tart pans and place a circle of pastry into each one. Bake for about five minutes, or until crisp, then remove from the oven and cool completely.

Once the pastry shells are cooled, remove them carefully from the pans.

Mix the garlic, mayonnaise, butter, and flat-leaf parsley together and season with salt and pepper.

Fill the baked pastry shells three-quarters full. Top each one with a covering made up of strips of *salami*, and serve.

Rotolini di bresaola alla rucola

Bresaola rolls with arugula

makes approx 30

14 oz fresh rocket leaves

3 oz freshly shaved parmesan

2 tbsp extra virgin olive oil

1 tbsp best-quality balsamic vinegar

salt and black pepper

20 slices of bresaola

This is so easy to make, using the wonderful cured beef of the Valtellina area of Lombardy, and some fresh rocket, plus a little fresh *parmesan* and just a dash of good-quality balsamic vinegar.

In a salad bowl, gently mix the rocket, *parmesan* shavings, olive oil, balsamic vinegar, and salt and pepper together to make a salad.

Lay the *bresaola* slices on a chopping board and divide the salad between all the slices more or less evenly.

Roll the slices up to encase the salad, sealing the two ends of the *bresaola* slice together with a little touch of olive oil, arrange on a serving dish and serve immediately.

PIEDMONT & AOSTA VALLEY

France and Switzerland both border the Alpine region of Piedmont, and both play a part in the culinary traditions of the region. Piedmont shares its Italian borders with Lombardy, Liguria, Emilia-Romagna, and Aosta Valley.

The main city of Torino is a city of interesting contrasts between the old world and the new. Torino is famous for its excellent artisan chocolate, which it has been making for centuries.

Somewhere between the ancient and the industrial lies a love of nature inherent to the Piedmontese. Because of the region's location and the mountains rising on three of its sides, Piedmont is home to a number of outstanding wooded parks and recreational areas.

The valleys and pasturelands, protected in part by the Alps, offer the ideal locations for growing grains like wheat, maize, and, most important of all, rice. The terraced hills of the Langhe lend themselves well to vineyards, and subsequently wine production. Garlic also grows effortlessly in the region, and is a very popular flavoring in everything from soups to meat dishes to pasta and beyond.

Freshwater fish and eels are very popular in Piedmontese cooking. Pork and pork products, as in most of Italy, are greatly treasured at the table, as are the excellent beef and veal that are produced here.

Dairy cattle thrive in Piedmont, and the dairy industry is strong, fostering a great love of cheese, cream, milk, and butter in everyone. The wide variety of cheeses produced in Piedmont derives mainly from cow's milk, though sheep's and goat's milks are sometimes added to alter flavor, texture, and color.

The Piedmontese also hold a particular fondness for game that is traditionally hunted in the wooded hills. The white truffle of Alba is one of the region's most important (and certainly most expensive) ingredients, adding distinctive flavor and earthiness to many recipes.

The region boasts precious grapevines that are mostly native, and the ancient vineyards produce many wines that are distinctive and unique to Piedmont.

Barolo, considered to be the "king of wines," traces its roots back past the time of Julius Caesar, who found the velvety red wine intriguing. With other wines like *barbera*, *dolcetto*, *gattinara*, *gavi*, *moscato d'Asti*, and *nebbiolo d'Alba* contributing to the Piedmontese wine tradition, the region is never without the perfect wine to serve alongside each plate in its wide range of dishes.

Italy's tiniest region, Aosta Valley, is tucked into the loftiest corner of the Alps with borders on France and Switzerland, neighbors who have always influenced the cooking of the largely French-speaking population. Still, though Aosta Valley shares traditions with Piedmont (of which it was long ago a province), the foods of its Alpine valleys have a character of their own.

Pasta and olive oil are almost novelties in a robust mountain cuisine that is firmly based on cheese and meat, rye bread, potatoes, *polenta*, *gnocchi*, *risotto*, and soups. Cows grazed on Alpine meadows provide fine butter and lots of local cheeses called *toma*, *robiola*, and above all the famous *fontina* DOP, which features in many a dish, including the local version of fondue called *fonduta*. Many local cheeses have been made in this valley since the fifteenth century. Cheese is also used with *polenta*, *risotto*, and in thick soups, whose ingredients range beyond the usual vegetables, meat, rice, and potatoes to include mushrooms, chestnuts, and almonds.

Right: Vineyards near Barolo, Piedmonte

Tartellete rustiche

Rustic tartlets

makes 15
small tartlets

²/₃ cup whole wheat
  flour

²/₃ cup all-purpose
  flour, plus extra for
  dusting

1 tsp superfine sugar

4–5 tbsp olive oil

1 egg yolk

1 tsp coarse-grain
  mustard

butter, for greasing

3 oz gorgonzola

2 tbsp heavy cream

salt and black pepper

1 carrot, finely sliced

1 small red onion,
  finely sliced

1 pear, finely sliced

1 celery heart, finely
  sliced

The combination of vegetables, pear, and *gorgonzola* in these little tartlets is really very special. You'll need tartlet tins to prepare these.

Put the flours, sugar, olive oil, egg yolk, and mustard into a bowl and rub everything together to form a mixture similar in texture to bread crumbs. Add just enough water to pull it all into a ball, then wrap in plastic wrap and chill in the refrigerator for at least 30 minutes.

Preheat the oven to 375°F. Roll the chilled pastry out on a lightly floured surface and cut into 15 circles the same size as your tartlet tins. Butter the tartlet tins, then dust with flour. Place the pastry circles into the tins, then line each with parchment paper and blind bake them. Remove from the oven and cool on a wire rack.

Stir the *gorgonzola* with the cream and salt and pepper until smooth, then place a small teaspoon of the *gorgonzola* in each cooled pastry case. Top with a few slices of carrot, onion, pear, and celery, and serve.

Polpettine di formaggio alle noci

Goat cheese balls with walnuts

serves 4

6 oz fresh, creamy
  goat cheese

¹/₂ cup walnuts,
  finely chopped

4 oz parmesan,
  grated

salt and black pepper

¹/₂ cup fresh bread
  crumbs

2 tbsp olive oil

7 oz baby salad leaves

A delicious and traditional dish from the city of Cuneo, and full of wonderful textures.

Blend the goat cheese with the chopped walnuts and the *parmesan*.

Season the mixture with salt and pepper to taste, then roll into cherry-sized balls. Roll again in the bread crumbs and flatten very slightly with the palm of your hand.

Heat the olive oil in a nonstick frying pan and fry the cheese balls for a couple of minutes on each side to turn them crisp and golden brown.

Scatter the salad leaves onto a serving dish, top with the cheese balls, and serve at once.

Left: Tartellete rustiche

Pandorato al formaggio

Golden cheese bread

serves 4

⅔ cup cold milk

4 oz fontina, or mixed cheeses

2 eggs

4 tbsp unsalted butter

salt and black pepper

1 large stale bread roll, sliced

4 tbsp all-purpose flour

¾ cups sunflower oil, for frying

This is a wonderfully golden, cheesy bread that is perfect with cured meats such as *salami*.

Pour about three-quarters of the milk into the bowl of a double-boiler and add the cheese. Separate the eggs.

Place the bowl over a pan of simmering water and melt the cheese into the milk, stirring frequently, then whisk in the egg yolks and stir in the butter. Keep the mixture warm but turn the heat off under the double-boiler.

Whisk the egg whites until stiff in a separate bowl, and season with salt and pepper.

Heat the oil in a wide frying pan until sizzling hot. Dip the sliced bread into the remaining milk, then into the flour, and finally into the egg whites, and then fry in the hot oil. Drain on paper towels and then arrange on a plate or serving dish. Pour the cheese over the bread and serve at once.

Tortino di patate e fontina

Savory potato cake with fontina

serves 8

8 medium potatoes

4 tbsp extra virgin olive oil

1 garlic clove

1 tsp dried thyme

7 oz fresh wild mushrooms

2 tbsp marsala

7 oz fontina, sliced

salt and black pepper

Boil the potatoes whole and unpeeled in salted water until tender, then drain, cool, and peel. Slice thinly.

Use some of the oil to grease an ovenproof dish, then line the bottom of the dish with the sliced potatoes, brush with oil, and set aside. Preheat the oven to 375°F.

Put the remaining oil in a pan with the garlic and the thyme. Heat together for about five minutes, then add the mushrooms and stir together. Cook for about 10 minutes, then add the *marsala*, and season. Continue to cook for another three or four minutes, then take off the heat.

Roast the potatoes in the oven for about 10 minutes, then cover with the mushrooms and the sliced cheese. Bake for a further 10 minutes, then remove from the oven, cut into neat squares or wedges, and serve at once.

Mezzelune ripiene di prosciutto cotto e fontina

Pastry crescents with ham and fontina

serves 8

1 packet of all-butter
   short-crust pastry

flour, for dusting

5 oz fontina, cubed

5 oz cooked ham,
   roughly chopped

butter, for greasing

sea salt

Flavors and textures come together perfectly in this combination of flaky pastry, salty ham, and creamy cheese.

Roll out the pastry evenly and thinly on a lightly floured surface, then cut into about 10 two-inch circles. Preheat the oven to 375°F.

Place a few cubes of cheese and about one teaspoon of chopped ham in the center of each circle of pastry, then fold over the circles to form a crescent shape.

Lay the crescents onto a well-buttered baking tray or several baking trays and sprinkle with salt.

Bake for 10 minutes and serve hot

Cipolle ripiene di magro

Baked stuffed onions

serves 6

3¾ cups water

salt

12 small, even-sized
onions, peeled

1 lb peeled pumpkin,
de-seeded and cut
into large chunks

4½ oz mostarda di
frutta plus syrup,
finely chopped

1 egg, beaten

¼ tsp grated nutmeg

1¼ cups amaretti
cookies, crushed

4 tbsp butter

Although these onions are traditionally served as a vegetable side dish
for a main course, they can also be served as part of an *antipasto* or as an
unusual sweet-and-sour-flavored *canapé*. The smaller the onions, the more
elegant the *canapé* will be.

Pour the water into a large, deep frying pan, add some salt, and bring to a boil. Drop in the
peeled onions and the pumpkin. Boil for about five minutes, or until the onions are about
three-quarters cooked. Take out the onions and leave in a colander to drain.

Continue to cook the pumpkin until really tender, then drain the pumpkin thoroughly,
squeeze dry in a clean cloth, and put into a bowl.

Add the *mostarda di frutta* and its syrup, egg, nutmeg, and *amaretti*. Mix all this together
very thoroughly.

Cut the onions in half from root to top. Take out the central core of the onions and discard.
Fill each onion half with the pumpkin stuffing and level the top. Dot each onion half with
butter. Preheat the oven to 400°F.

Butter a baking dish thoroughly with the remaining butter and then place the stuffed
onions in the dish. Bake for 30 minutes, or until the onions are cooked through. Serve hot
or cold.

Focaccia di patate

Potato focaccia

serves 8

2 large potatoes

3½ oz all-purpose flour

1½ oz fresh yeast,
dissolved in 6 tbsp of
very warm water

¼ cup extra virgin
olive oil

sea salt

2 tbsp chopped fresh
rosemary

salami, to serve (if
desired)

This substantial bread is perfect when served thinly sliced with cheese.

Boil the potatoes in salted water until tender, then drain and peel while they are still hot.
Push them through a food mill or ricer to create a very smooth purée.

Knead the mashed potato purée into the flour with the dissolved yeast, and enough extra
water to create a smooth, elastic dough that will not stick to the counter surface or your hands.

Place the dough into a lightly oiled bowl, and leave the *focaccia* to rise in a warm place,
covered with a cloth, for about an hour or until doubled in volume.

Tip the dough out onto the work surface, press it into a well-oiled shallow baking tray, and
sprinkle with salt and rosemary. Add a final drizzle of oil and bake for 25 to 30 minutes until
cooked through and with a crisp top and bottom.

Remove from the baking tray and serve warm with more olive oil for dipping, or cut it
into bite-sized sandwiches filled with a slice or two of *salami*.

Right: Focaccia di patate

Fonduta alla Piedmontese

Piedmontese cheese fondue

serves 4

1 lb fontina, cubed

1 tbsp all-purpose flour or fine polenta flour

¾ cup cold milk

4 egg yolks

4 oz butter

This is the Italian version of a classic cheese *fondue*, as made in Piedmont and Aosta Valley. It will make great party food, or it can be used to dress pasta or to make a *risotto*.

In a deep stainless steel pot, mix the cheese and the flour together thoroughly. Pour the milk into the pot and leave to soften for 30 minutes, then drain and discard the milk.

Put the egg yolks and butter into the top half of a double-boiler with the cheese and stir until the cheese has melted. The eggs must be allowed to thicken slowly and gently.

As soon as the *fonduta* is velvety smooth and piping hot, serve it in warmed bowls with slices of toasted or fried bread, *grissini* (bread sticks), or small squares of fried or grilled *polenta*.

Crostini di polenta ai funghi

Polenta crostini with mushrooms and cheese

makes 12 crostini

4 4 × 8-inch slices of cooked, cold polenta, about 1 in thick (see page 16)

5 tbsp extra virgin olive oil

14 oz mixed mushrooms

2 garlic cloves, crushed

salt and black pepper

5 oz fontina, rind removed and cubed

4 tbsp milk

2 tsp finely chopped flat-leaf parsley

This is a great way to use up leftover *polenta*, but you could also use thin slices of crusty bread if you prefer.

Cut the big *polenta* slices into thirds so that you end up with 12 neat, small slices. Heat half the oil in a nonstick pan and fry the *polenta* slices for about five minutes on each side or until crisp and golden. Keep the fried slices warm in a low oven.

Cut the mushrooms into even-sized pieces about the size of a broad bean.

Heat the remaining oil in a frying pan with the garlic until the garlic begins to turn golden brown, then discard the garlic and add the mushrooms. Season with salt and pepper and cook gently until soft, about 15 minutes.

Put the cubed cheese in the bowl of a double-boiler, cover with the milk, and place over a pan of simmering water to melt completely, stirring occasionally.

Arrange the warm *polenta* on a platter, spoon over the mushrooms, cover with melted cheese, and sprinkle with parsley to serve.

Right: Fonduta alla Piedmontese

TRENTINO ALTO ADIGE

Trentino Alto Adige is located in the northeast of Italy and stretches right across the Dolomites. This mountainous region is home to scented pine forests, crystal-clear alpine lakes, and gently rolling, vine-covered hills that lead down to the plains of the Veneto. The most striking natural feature of the region has to be the Dolomites, which are the very essence of the region. The Dolomites are a designated UNESCO World Heritage Site and offer an unforgettable experience for lovers of skiing and other winter sports.

Possibly the most fundamental element of Trentino cuisine is *polenta*, which consists of ground cornmeal boiled and stirred for a long time in salted water until thickened, when it forms a kind of porridge. There are, however, many different and delicious ways to enjoy it. It is often served with local cheeses, a game stew, *baccala'*, or beans. And it is often still cooked over an open fire, so that the burning wood adds a slightly smoky taste to the *polenta* bubbling away in the pot. By mixing in ground, dark saracen corn, basic *polenta* takes on another flavor altogether and becomes dark enough to be called *polenta nera*, or black *polenta*. Freshwater fish, pork, game, milk, vegetables, and fruit used in both sweet and savory dishes also shape the basic themes of the simple, local cuisine.

Canederli are one of the most important specialties of the northern Alto Adige region. *Canederli* are large dumplings made out of stale bread, eggs, flour, and milk, which then have other ingredients such as bacon, *salami*, and green vegetables like cabbage or spinach added to the basic mixture. Usually served as a filling *antipasto* or as a first course, they are poached in a clear broth or

water. Sometimes they are served alongside a stew, and by putting a prune into the center and then dipping them in bread crumbs before simmering in water, local cooks make a sweet version. Other dumpling-type dishes include *spätzle*, made with flour, eggs, and salt, and the very popular *spinatspätzle*, made with spinach. These are like small *gnocchi*, and are often served alongside a stew like the famous local *goulash*.

Cakes and pastries play an important role here in this cold climate. Favorites include *strudel* (often filled with apples spiced with cinnamon) or the rather doughy *zelten*, (filled with walnuts and dried fruits). Other desserts echo those of the Veneto, with names that are almost the same and recipes that vary only very slightly. The wild berries, which grow in the woods and meadows of the region, are widely used in the local desserts, as well as being added to delicious liqueurs.

The lively street market in Trento overflows with wonderful local produce, especially in the summer and fall. The wide range of varieties from the Val di Non and elsewhere can be found here, as can some of the 250 types of wild mushrooms found in the mountains and hills.

Dishes of cold cuts, mainly pork, are very popular here, and are often served as an *antipasto* with cheese, pickled gherkins, and vegetables, as well as beer and *sauerkraut*. Very warming in the winter are the traditional, hearty soups often thickened with barley and flavored with bacon or *speck*. Also popular is the local version of the Swiss *rösti*, called *grostl* in this region, a deliciously crispy pancake of potatoes and bacon.

Right: Winter Promenade, Merano, Trentino Alto Adige

Tortellini coi crauti (krauttörtchen)

Tortellini with sauerkraut

serves 6

Here's an unusual way to enjoy *sauerkraut*!

1 quantity basic pizza
  dough (see page 128)

flour, for dusting

6 paper-thin slices
  of cured ham

2 hard-boiled eggs,
  shelled and cut into
  rounds

1 cup sauerkraut

1 tsp cumin seeds

unsalted butter

mustard, to serve

Roll out the *pizza* dough as thinly as possible and cut into 24 evenly sized circles.

Cut the ham slices in half and lay half a slice on top of 12 circles of dough.

Place a slice of hard-boiled egg on top of each circle of dough, top with a spoonful of *sauerkraut*, and sprinkle with cumin seeds.

Butter a large baking tray (or several trays) thoroughly, and pre-heat the oven to 450°F. Cover the filled dough circles with the remaining rolled out circles and press the edges closed very carefully, using the tines of a fork and a little water to help seal them. Transfer the filled disks onto the buttered baking trays and bake for about 10 minutes, or until golden brown.

Remove from the oven and serve hot, with mustard offered on the side.

Torta di cipolle, ricotta e speck

Savory ricotta, onion, and speck pie

This pie is sure to delight lovers of cheese, vegetables, and meat.

serves 8 to 10
as a canapé

3½ cups all-purpose
  flour, plus extra for
  dusting

5 tbsp olive oil, plus
  extra for greasing

14 oz white onions,
  finely sliced

4 tbsp unsalted butter

4 eggs, beaten

7 oz speck, finely sliced

8 oz ricotta

3 oz parmesan,
  freshly grated

salt and black pepper

Knead together the flour, two tablespoons of the oil, and a little water to make a smooth ball of dough. Divide into quarters and cover, then leave to rest for about an hour at room temperature.

Fry the onion in the rest of the oil and the butter until softened, for about 20 minutes. Leave to cool. Preheat the oven to 375°F.

Once the onions are cool, stir them into the beaten eggs. Add the *speck*, *ricotta*, and *parmesan*. Season with salt and pepper. Stir until thick and well blended.

Roll out the four pieces of dough as thinly as possible and oil a suitably sized cake pan or baking dish. Cut the rolled-out pastry into equally sized disks to fit.

Lay two of the disks of dough on the bottom, brushing them both with oil. Cover with the *ricotta* and onion mixture and then lay the second disk on top. Brush with oil, cover with the final disk, brush again with oil, and then bake for about 35 minutes, or until crisp. Serve warm, sliced into small wedges.

Right: Torta di cipolle, ricotta e speck

Panini alle cipolle (zwiebelbrötchen)

Onion bread rolls

makes 10
small rolls

½ oz fresh yeast

1 tsp superfine sugar

2¾ cups all-purpose
flour

2 cups rye flour

1 tsp ground cumin

salt

1 onion, thinly sliced

1 tbsp unsalted butter

1 egg, beaten

The blend of cumin-scented flours create a good base for the butter-fried onions.

Blend the yeast in a small bowl with about half a cup of warm water, then add the sugar and a handful of all-purpose flour, and stir gently. Leave to stand in a warm place for 30 minutes.

After this time, when the yeast has become active, stir in the rest of the all-purpose flour, rye flour, cumin, salt, and as much water as is required to make a smooth, elastic ball of dough. Knead vigorously for 10 minutes, then place in an oiled bowl, covered, and leave to rise in a warm spot for two to three hours.

Meanwhile, fry the onion in the butter until softened and golden brown. Season with salt and set aside.

Punch down the risen dough, and shape into 10 small rolls. Preheat the oven to 400°F.

Lay the rolls on well-oiled baking trays and brush with the beaten egg, then press a small amount of the fried onions on top of each roll.

Bake for about 15 minutes before serving with butter and *speck*.

Insalata di funghi freschi

Fresh mushroom salad

serves 8

10 oz mushrooms

5 oz parmesan
shavings

3 tbsp extra virgin
olive oil

juice of ½ lemon

3 tbsp finely chopped
flat-leaf parsley

salt and white pepper

This makes a delightful and very light *canapé*, and can be served on spoons in elegant mouthful-sized quantities.

Clean and trim the mushrooms and slice them into very thin slices. Mix gently with the *parmesan* shavings.

Whisk together the oil, lemon juice, parsley, salt, and white pepper in a small bowl. Drizzle the dressing over the mushrooms and *parmesan* and serve at once.

Left: Panini alle cipolle (zwiebelbrötchen)

FRIULI VENEZIA GIULIA

With Slovenia on its eastern border and Austria to the north, it is not at all surprising to taste the influences of both these countries in the cuisine of Friuli Venezia Giulia. Spices such as paprika, poppy seeds, cinnamon, cumin, and horseradish are often used, and rice and *polenta* are very common, served instead of pasta. There are wonderful local sausages, and of course one cannot overlook the delicious ham from San Daniele, in the province of Udine, which rivals the best Parma ham in terms of flavor and quality. The region is also known for its delicious smoked ham, *speck*, produced here and also in neighboring Trentino Alto Adige.

Because of its historical connection with the Austro-Hungarian Empire, the cuisine of Friuli Venezia Giulia still has a great many Mitteleuropean influences, for example: their love of *sauerkraut*, savory and sweet *strudels* including a local boiled variation called *strucolo*, potatoes and turnips, and the tradition of lightly smoked meat, especially *prosciutto*. An obvious characteristic of the cooking of this region is the lack of tomatoes, and although they may sometimes be used, they are certainly nowhere near as important as they are farther south.

Friuli Venezia Giulia is also known for its wide use of barley, and the locals use this grain instead of rice to make their *orzotti*, similar to a *risotto*. There is an abundance of wild feathered and furred game in the inland areas, and the region also produces some very good beef.

This region produces many of the best Italian white wines, many of which are flowery and light and are made with Germanic grape varieties such as *riesling* and *muller thurgau*. It is also very proud of *picolit*, an extraordinary sweet wine developed in the 1700s, when a raging war kept a precious Hungarian wine called *tokay* from reaching Europe's courts.

In addition to their famous sweet and savory *strudels*, Friuli Venezia Giulia boasts many other cakes, including *gubana*, a spicy sweetbread with flavored with *grappa*.

The hearty, winter warming soups of Friuli (the most famous being *la jota*) are usually based on beans, greens, and pig's ribs, with a base of pork fat. Then there is the local specialty of *frico*, which is seasoned, salty local cheese, cut into pieces and fried in plenty of butter. This is sometimes served with *polenta*, but can also be served on its own as a snack.

The cooking from the city of Trieste and the town of Grado strongly reflects the Venetian style of seafood, but blended with the region's Austrian and Slavic influences. Here, the specialties are the local *brodetto*, a fish soup made with pieces of various locally caught fish, and *mesta*, a kind of *polenta* cooked in water and milk that is eaten with fish.

Right: Historical centre of Collio, Friuli Venezia Giulia

Torta rustica di speck e asparagi

Speck and asparagus tart

serves 8

1 lb 8 oz asparagus

8 oz short-crust pastry

oil for greasing

4 oz speck, cut into strips

½ cup ready-prepared béchamel sauce (see page 60)

4 oz freshly grated parmesan

Make this dish with the best of the season's asparagus. You won't regret the wait for this tender, flavorsome vegetable to make an appearance.

Trim the asparagus stalks and steam for about nine minutes, then cool and slice thinly lengthwise.

Preheat the oven to 300°F.

Roll out the pastry and use it to line a well-greased pie pan. Blind bake the pastry for about 10 minutes, then remove from the oven to cool.

Scatter the asparagus into the pastry, then add the *speck* and cover with the *béchamel*. Finally sprinkle with the *parmesan* and then bake for about 20 minutes before serving hot, in small slices.

Strudel salato

Savory strudel

makes 1 strudel

1 small, tender Savoy cabbage, washed and shredded

¼ cup extra virgin olive oil, plus extra for greasing

4 garlic cloves, finely chopped

1 tbsp finely chopped flat-leaf parsley

8 oz ricotta

1 packet of all-butter short-crust pastry

flour, for dusting

Here is a very traditional recipe from this region in the far northeast of the country.

Boil the cabbage until tender in salted water, then drain and squeeze dry. Chop it roughly and then sauté the cabbage in a frying pan with the oil, garlic, and parsley for about eight minutes. Remove from the heat and leave to cool, then mix with the *ricotta*.

Preheat the oven to 300°F. On a flour-dusted surface, roll out the pastry as finely as possible, then cover with the cabbage and *ricotta* mixture, leaving a clear rim around the edges.

Roll the pastry up to enclose the filling and seal the edges securely. Lay onto a well-oiled baking tray and bake for about 45 minutes before serving warm, in thin slices.

Right: Torta rustica di speck e asparagi

Fegatini alla Triestina

Chicken livers in the Trieste style

serves 6 to 8

1 onion, finely sliced

¼ cup extra virgin
   olive oil

6 juniper berries,
   lightly crushed

1 lb chicken livers,
   carefully cleaned

salt and black pepper

¾ cup red wine

From the wind-blown port city of Trieste comes this marvelous recipe for chicken livers, used to top toasted bread or *polenta* slices for a delicious *canapé*.

Fry the onion gently with the oil and the juniper berries for about five minutes, stirring frequently.

Add the chicken livers, season with salt and pepper, and pour over the wine. Cook quickly, turning the livers for about five to six minutes, then serve on top of toasted bread or small slices of fried or grilled *polenta*.

Mandorle speziato

Spiced almonds

serves 4 to 6

1 tsp olive oil

1⅓ cups blanched
   almonds

coarse sea salt

¼ tsp smoked paprika

Sometimes the simplest recipes are the most satisfying! Paprika is a real favorite in this region, and it goes so well with local almonds.

Heat the olive oil in a non-stick skillet, then add the almonds and toss over the heat for about 5 minutes until golden.

Use a slotted spoon to transfer the nuts to a bowl, leaving as much oil in the pan as possible. Sprinkle the nuts generously with coarse sea salt and the paprika, and toss the nuts to coat them in the seasoning. Leave to cool then transfer to a serving dish.

Right: Fegatini alla Triestina

LE MARCHE

Le Marche makes the most of both the bounty of the Adriatic and the produce of the land. Thanks to the port of Ancona, the region has also had access to ingredients from faraway countries. There is something unmistakably joyous about the preparation and consumption of food in this region, a sense of tremendous pleasure derived from the traditional dishes and their consumption. Le Marche represents a sort of meeting point between the gastronomy of the north and that of the south. Lying as it does in the center of the country, this verdant region has upheld a great tradition of gastronomy and hospitality. The coastline, the mountains, and the soft rolling countryside are a real blessing to this beautiful region.

The local cuisine is dominated by strong flavors and many much-loved meat recipes, especially the rich, roasted pork dish called *porchetta*, stuffed spit roast pork with fennel, garlic, and olive oil. Favorite meats include veal, rabbit, game birds, chicken, and goose.

The local fish soup, which is more of a stew, is known as *brodetto*. This is the most famous fish dish of the Adriatic coast and recipes vary from one coastal town to another, even within a few miles. *Brodetto* traditionally includes red and gray mullet, cuttlefish or squid, garlic, and saffron, and it is served on a bed of fried or toasted bread. Other seafood favorites include *stoccafisso* (air-dried salt cod) from the port of Ancona and other recipes using locally caught and prized fish and seafood.

Another of the most typical regional specialties is the traditional recipe for fat, juicy olives, which are served stuffed with a meat filling, rolled in flour, egg, and bread crumbs and finally deep-fried. History tells us the ancient Romans enjoyed these extra-large green olives, which are unique to this area. Also worth a very special mention is the delicious *prosciutto di Carpegna*, which, like *San Daniele* and *Parma*, benefits from being cured in a small area in the hills near the coastline, cured by a microclimate that ensures unique and very special results.

Vincisgrassi, the famous *lasagne* of Le Marche, comes in many versions, including with ground pork, mushrooms, tomato, and *béchamel* sauce. Another is made with with strips of pigeon breast and *marsala*, but they are always made with the precious local black truffles. It is said that this dish was created by adding extra ingredients to the standard Bolognese *ragu* to impress a German general called Windisch Graetz who was put in charge of the area during the Austro-Hungarian rule of the late 1700s.

Pecorino, particularly soft, young *pecorino*, made from the local ewe's milk, is the favorite cheese of Le Marche. Desserts in this region are usually not overwhelmingly sweet and often use *ricotta* as an ingredient, such as *calcioni* and *piconi*, for example. Other desserts include a *pizza dolce*, or sweet pizza, and *frustenga*, a deliciously rich fruit and nut cake. Alcoholic drinks typical of this region include a local *grappa* and various other homemade infused liqueurs, but the most popular is *mistra'* (named after the Mistral wind), which is an aniseed liqueur used as a digestive and which is also added to some desserts.

The wines of Le Marche include several full-bodied DOC reds like Ancona's *rosso conero*, the very popular *rosso piceno*, and the sparkling and wonderfully named *vernaccia di serrapetrona*. The real winner in terms of the wines of the region is *verdicchio* (*dei castelli di iesi* or *di matelica*), which is considered by many to be the best wine to enjoy with seafood.

Right: Piazza del Popolo, Ascoli Piceno, Le Marche

Olive all'Ascolana

Stuffed and deep-fried green olives

makes 60

60 giant (queen)
  green olives
  preserved in brine

¼ lb pork fat

¼ cup extra virgin
  olive oil

5½ oz ground pork

¼ lb ground beef

1 tbsp tomato paste,
  diluted in a little
  cold water

3 chicken livers,
  chopped

3 tbsp fresh white
  bread crumbs

3 tbsp beef stock

1 egg, beaten

1¾ oz parmesan,
  grated

pinch of grated
  nutmeg

salt and black pepper

5 tbsp all-purpose
  flour

2 eggs beaten with a
  splash of milk

3–4 tbsp fine, dried
  bread crumbs

oil, for deep-frying

lemon wedges,
  to garnish

This is perhaps the most famous of all the specialties of this rich region on the Adriatic coast.

Pit all the olives carefully with an appropriate instrument to keep them whole and as neat as possible. Set aside.

Fry the pork fat with the oil and the ground pork and beef until the meat is well browned, then add the tomato paste. Mix together and cook for 20 minutes, then add the chicken livers and cook for another 10 minutes.

Cool the mixture then chop finely with a heavy knife, or put the mixture into a food processor and process until smooth.

Add the fresh bread crumbs, stock, beaten egg, and *parmesan* and combine. Season to taste with nutmeg, salt, and pepper.

Carefully fill each olive with this mixture. Roll the olives in flour, then in the egg and milk mixture, and then in bread crumbs. Heat a wok or large, heavy-based pan containing the oil. When it starts to smoke, drop a crust of bread in. If the oil starts to froth around the bread and the bread turns golden, it is ready and you can start frying the olives in batches. Drain on paper towels, and serve hot or cold with the lemon wedges.

Tortino di acciughe con verdura

Savory cake with anchovies and vegetables

serves 6

20 fresh anchovies

5 oz raw spinach

2 garlic cloves

4 tbsp extra virgin
   olive oil, plus extra
   for greasing

6 asparagus

2 zucchini

salt and black pepper

1 packet of all-butter
   short-crust pastry

The anchovies bring the vegetables in this dish alive.
Use only fresh, in-season asparagus and zucchini.

Gut and clean the anchovies, removing the spine and bones. Wash
and pat dry.

Chop the spinach leaves, then place them in a wide frying
pan with five tablespoons of water, a whole garlic clove, and two
tablespoons of extra virgin olive oil. Cook for five minutes, then
take off the heat and leave to cool.

Wash and trim the asparagus, cut off the tips, slice the stems
into rounds, and steam the tips only for four minutes until tender.
Set aside.

In another pan, sauté the sliced asparagus stems, the zucchini,
the second whole garlic clove, and the rest of the oil. Cook until
everything is tender, season, and then set aside to cool. Preheat the
oven to 400°F.

Blind bake the pastry in a large, shallow pie pan as directed on
the packet. Remove the pan from the oven and lay the anchovies
on the bottom. Cover with the vegetables (discarding the garlic
cloves) and then lay the asparagus spears on top. Drizzle with a
final spoonful of extra virgin olive oil and bake for about 15 minutes
before serving.

Piconi al pecorino

Pastry crescents with pecorino

serves 6

3 cups all-purpose
flour, plus extra for
dusting

⅔ cup superfine sugar

14 tbsp unsalted
butter, cubed

4 egg yolks

zest of 1 large,
unwaxed lemon

14 oz mild pecorino,
grated

2 egg whites

1 egg

salt and black pepper

1 egg yolk, beaten

oil, for greasing

These are truly delicious, especially if served with a little drizzle
of honey to finish them off.

Pile the flour and sugar onto the work surface, and make a hollow in the center
of the flour. Add the butter, egg yolks, and half the lemon zest.

Quickly knead this together to form a soft pastry dough, then wrap it in
plastic wrap and place it somewhere cool for about 30 minutes.

In a separate bowl, blend the *pecorino* with the remaining lemon zest, the
egg whites, the whole egg, and seasoning. This should result in a fairly thick
mixture.

Roll out the pastry on a lightly floured surface and cut into circles with a
diameter of about one-and-a-half inches, and preheat the oven to 375°F.

Place a teaspoonful of the filling into the center of each circle of dough, fold
them in half, and seal tightly with the beaten egg yolk.

Cut a small cross on top of each of these *piconi*, then lay them all on a well-
oiled baking tray and brush lightly with any remaining egg yolk.

Bake for about 10 minutes or until golden and crisp. Serve hot or cold.

Alici marinate al limone

Anchovies marinated in lemon

serves 8

3 lb fresh anchovies

thinly sliced peel, no pith, of 1 unwaxed lemon

2 dried bay leaves

2 tbsp finely chopped flat-leaf parsley

3 cups white wine vinegar

3 tbsp extra virgin olive oil

There is no mistaking the lovely, sharp taste of this marinade. At once sour and lemony, it will wake up your palate and appetite.

Clean and gut the anchovies, removing the spine and bones, and washing thoroughly. Pat them dry.

Lay the anchovies in a bowl with the lemon peel, bay leaves, and parsley.

Pour the vinegar into a saucepan, bring to a boil, and then pour it, boiling hot, over the anchovies. Leave to cool and marinate for four hours.

When you are ready to serve, remove the anchovies from the vinegar, draining them carefully.

Arrange the anchovies on a platter, drizzle with the olive oil, and serve.

Cannelli arrosto

Roasted razor clams

serves 8

2 lb live razor clams

6 oz fresh bread crumbs

1 ripe tomato, cubed

2 garlic cloves, finely chopped

2 tbsp extra virgin olive oil

salt and black pepper

2 tbsp finely chopped fresh flat-leaf parsley

These are truly delicious, but do warn your guests that the shells will get very hot.

Wash the razor clams and steam them open quickly. Remove the sand sac and prise the flesh away from the shell so that it all sits on one of the two shells. Pre heat the oven to 375°F.

In a bowl, mix together the bread crumbs, cubed tomato, garlic, and olive oil. Season with salt and pepper.

Use this mixture to fill the empty shelll and then sandwich the shells back together.

Arrange the filled shells in a baking dish and drizzle with olive oil. Bake in the oven for about eight minutes. Sprinkle with parsley and serve hot.

Left: Alici marinate al limone

Index

Picture credits

All images by Colin Dutton, 4 Corners Images with the exception of:

Page 115 © Rafael Zwiegincew/Getty Images
Page 192 © StockFood
Pages 155, 159, 165, 168, 182, 209, 211, cover © Ian Garlick